MESSAGE OF BIBLICAL SPIRITUALITY
Editorial Director: Carolyn Osiek, RSCJ

Volume 13

Letters in the
Pauline Tradition

Ephesians, Colossians,
I Timothy, II Timothy and Titus

Carol L. Stockhausen

Michael Glazier
Wilmington, Delaware

About the Author
Carol K. Stockhausen received her Ph.D. in Religious Studies from Marquette University. She is currently an Assistant Professor of Theology at Marquette, and is a member of numerous learned societies including the Catholic Biblical Association and the Society of Biblical Literature. Her major scholarly interests are in the Pauline and Synoptic traditions.

First published in 1989 by Michael Glazier, Inc. 1935 West Fourth Street, Wilmington, Delaware 19805.

Library of Congress Cataloging-in-Publication Data

Stockhausen, Carol L.
    Letters in the Pauline tradition: Ephesians, Colossians, and I Timothy, II Timothy and Titus/by Carol L. Stockhausen.
        p.   cm.—(Message of biblical spirituality; v. 13)
    Bibliography: p.
    Includes index.
    ISBN: 0-89453-563-3.—ISBN: 0-89453-579-X (pbk.)
    1. Bible. N.T. Ephesians—Criticism, interpretation, etc.
2. Bible. N.T. Colossians—Criticism, interpretation, etc.
3. Bible. N.T. Pastoral Epistles—Criticism, interpretation, etc.
4. Spiritual life—Biblical teaching.   I. Title. II. Series.
BS2695.6.S65S76   1989
227—dc19   89-30676
                                                                              CIP
Cover Design by Florence Bern
Printed in the United States of America by Edwards Brothers

Table of Contents

EDITOR'S PREFACE

One of the characteristics of church life today is a revived interest in spirituality. There is a growing list of resources in this area, yet the need for more is not exhausted. People are yearning for guidance in living an integrated life of faith in which belief, attitude, affections, prayer, and action form a cohesive unity which gives meaning to their lives.

The biblical tradition is a rich resource for the variety of ways in which people have heard God's call to live a life of faith and fidelity. In each of the biblical books we have a witness to the initiative of God in human history and to the attempts of people not so different from ourselves to respond to the revelation of God's love and care.

The fifteen volumes in the *Message of Biblical Spirituality* series aim to provide ready access to the treasury of biblical faith. Modern social science has made us aware of how the particular way in which one views reality conditions the ways in which one will interpret experience and life itself. Each volume in this series is an attempt to retell and interpret the biblical story from within the faith perspective that originally formed it. Each seeks to portray what it is like to see God, the world, and oneself from a particular point of view and to search for ways to respond faithfully to that vision. We who are citizens of our twentieth century world cannot be people of the ancient biblical world, but we can grow closer to their experience and their faith and thus closer to God, through the living Word of God which is the Bible.

The series includes an international group of authors representing England, Ireland, Canada, and the United States, but whose life experience has included first-hand knowledge of many other countries. All are proven scholars and committed believers whose faith is as important to them as their scholarship. Each acts as interpreter of one part of the biblical tradition in order to enable its spiritual vitality to be passed on to others. It is our hope that through their labor the reader will be able to enter more deeply into the life of faith, hope, and love through a fuller understanding of and appreciation for the biblical Word as handed down to us by God's faithful witnesses, the biblical authors themselves.

Carolyn Osiek, RSCJ
Associate Professor of New Testament Studies
Catholic Theological Union, Chicago

Introduction

The title of this volume not only describes its contents but also hints at the presuppositions which have informed the writing of it. Five letters will be discussed here—the epistles addressed to the Colossians, to the Ephesians, two to the disciple Timothy and one to Titus. Scholars do not agree about their authorship. Many experts in the field of New Testament studies think that it is very unlikely that the letters addressed to the individuals Timothy and Titus were written by the Apostle Paul himself. Fewer scholars, but still a majority of those who study the letter, think that the Epistle to the Ephesians is also pseudonymous, that is, written by someone else under the name of the famous Apostle to the Gentiles. Opinion is more evenly divided regarding the Epistle to the Colossians. Many scholars assume that it was written by Paul himself, but a significant number argue that Colossians too was written by a disciple of Paul (possibly the same Epaphras who is mentioned in Col 1:7 and 4:12).[1]

---

[1]For a discussion of the phenomenon of pseudonymity and of the pseudonymous authorship of the letters to be treated here, you might consult the following works: Kurt Aland, "The Problem of Anonymity and Pseudonymity in Christian Literature of the First Two Centuries," *Journal of Theological Studies* n.s. 12 (1961) pp. 39-49 (a scholarly and classic presentation of the issues); Leander E. Keck and Victor Paul

Although no absolute certainty is possible concerning the authorship of any of these five letters, for the sake of clarity a decision must be made on the issue. The viewpoint taken on this question influences interpretation of the letters at a fundamental level. In this volume, a decision has been made in favor of pseudonymity. In my opinion—and it remains just that, a scholarly judgment rather than a statement of absolute fact—all of the letters which I will discuss here were written by disciples of the Apostle Paul following his death.

Pseudonymity, or writing in the name of another, was very common in the ancient world from which these letters come and did not carry with it the implication of dishonesty or fraud that such an act usually has in our culture. For example, the pupil or disciple of a great philosopher or rabbi might compose works in the name of the master as a way of continuing a teaching tradition, with no intention to deceive. Such a practice would lend authority to the new book as a legitimate representative of a revered tradition, while at the same time contributing to the development of that tradition through time. It is just this impulse which was at work in the composition of Colossians, Ephesians and the Pastoral Epistles.

The consequences of such a viewpoint for the interpretation of these letters are important. First, if the Apostle Paul himself did

Furnish, *The Pauline Letters.* Interpreting Biblical Texts. (Nashville: Abingdon Press, 1984), especially pp. 48-62; J Paul Sampley, Joseph Burgess, Gerhard Krodel, Reginald H. Fuller, *Ephesians, Colossians, 2 Thessalonians, The Pastoral Epistles.* Proclamation Commentaries. (Philadelphia: Fortress Press, 1978), especially pp. 9-12, 41, 69-71, 97-103 (which understand these letters to be pseudo-Pauline); and Luke T. Johnson, *The Writings of the New Testament,* (Philadelphia: Fortress Press, 1986), pp. 357-359, 367-372, 381-389 and bibliographical notes suggesting further reading which has a strong preference for the authenticity of the letters).

not write these letters and yet they are written in his name, we can assume that Paul himself and his thought, such as we can find it expressed in his authentic letters which are preserved, are the inspiration and source for the theology of these later works placed so consciously into his tradition and under his authority. For, while the Pauline authorship of our letters may be doubted, their character as representatives of a Pauline way of thinking cannot. Second, although a relationship to Paul's own theology may be presumed, a resemblance between Paul's own situation and that of the author of any of our pseudonymous letters cannot. Third, because Ephesians, Colossians and the letters to Timothy and Titus were not written by Paul and, therefore, their actual authors are unknown to us, we have no right to assume that any of these letters was written by the same person as any of the others. As a consequence, we cannot assume that the situation and concerns of one of our letters are identical, or even similar, to those of the others.

This last consideration is especially important for this particular volume. One of the goals of the Message of Biblical Spirituality series is to enable its readers to walk in the world of a particular New Testament writer and to feel what it would be like to live as a Christian within that universe of meaning, experience and emotion. In the case of this volume, therefore, we will be dealing with at least two different worlds, neither of them the same as that presupposed in the letters of Paul himself. Our study will be all the more fascinating and rewarding for that, however, as we will be able to observe and enter into the experience of several very early believers as they develop Paul's preaching of Christ in new directions in response to different perceptions of the universe in which they lived and changing events in the life of a church moving into the future.

This volume falls naturally into two parts, although of unequal size, the first dealing with the Epistles to the Colossians and Ephesians and the second with the Pastoral Epistles. Before beginning Part One, the reader should read quickly through Colossians and Ephesians to set the stage upon which the Christians of Colossae and Ephesus may reveal themselves to us. They are Christians indeed very much like Christians today, united with us in a common belief in the death and resurrection of Jesus Christ for the salvation of those who believe in him. But they lived in a world very different from ours. Into that world I now invite you to walk.

Part One
The Epistles to the Colossians and to the Ephesians

1

The Relationship Between the Epistles

There is good reason to treat these two letters together. Although differences between them do exist and we will be aware of these when they are important to the focus of this discussion, even a cursory reading of Colossians and Ephesians reveals that the two letters bear some sort of relationship to each other. Look back to the letters themselves and compare, for example, Ephesians 6:21-22 and Colossians 4:7-8. In these small texts, of little theological interest for us here, we can nevertheless see the closest of many cases of parallel wording in the letters. There are numerous and significant theological parallels also. Compare, for example, the view of Christ and his church present in Colossians 2:17-19 and Ephesians 4:15-16. Read first one of these texts and then the other.[2] Notice that the context, in both cases, is a warning against

---

[2] If you are interested in studying the Pauline letter corpus as a literary and theological whole and as an aid to reading parallel passages in studying the present volume, I recommend an extremely useful research tool. *Pauline Parallels*, Second Edition. ed. Fred O. Francis and J. Paul Sampley (Philadelphia: Fortress Press, 1984) provides "a sequential presentation of each of the ten chief letters attributed to Paul," (p. xi) divided into paragraphs and numbered consecutively from Romans through Philemon. The Pastoral Epistles are not included. On each page, then, one finds set out in vertical columns the most significant parallels to each Pauline passage.

false teaching of some kind—"No one is free, therefore, to pass judgment on you in terms of what you eat or drink or what you do on yearly or monthly feasts, or on the sabbath." (Col 2:16), and "Let us, then, be children no longer, tossed here and there, carried about by every wind of doctrine that originates in human trickery and skill in proposing error." (Eph 4:14).[3] The warning in Ephesians is much less specific than that of Colossians and seems to refer to doctrinal, rather than ritual, error. Yet the teaching about Christ which is opposed to false teaching is nearly identical in each case. The underlying christological idea is the *body of Christ* (Col 2:17/Eph 4:12), an idea that is very important in both of these Pauline letters, as we shall see. Yet there is very little explanation of this well-known Pauline metaphor. For a full explanation of the idea of the church as Christ's body we need to look to the place in Paul's own letters where the comparison first appears, I Corinthians 12. In Ephesians and Colossians, only two aspects of the idea of the church as Christ's body are stressed, and the same ones—the *growth* of the body (the church) and the single *source* of this growth in the *head* of that body (Christ). It is fascinating to read and re-read these two small sections of Colossians and Ephesians in the light of I Corinthians 12-14 to see how they catch and express the essence of Paul's message, but for now we need only notice the strikingly similar use these two pseudonymous epistles have made of the theological concept of the body of Christ.

The nature of Christian existence is also expressed in an unmistakably similar way in Colossians 3:9-10 and Ephesians 4:23-24. Again the contexts are not unrelated. This time a warning

---

[3]All texts cited in this volume are taken from *The New American Bible*. Catholic Biblical Association of America. (New York: P. J. Kenedy & Sons, 1970).

against immorality introduces a profound teaching about the transformation of human existence which occurs when Christians die with Christ in baptism—"Put to death whatever in your nature is rooted in earth: fornication, uncleanness, passion, evil desires, and that lust which is idolatry." (Col 3:5) and "I declare and solemnly attest in the Lord that you must no longer live as the pagans do . . . without remorse they have abandoned themselves to lust and the indulgence of every sort of lewd conduct." (Eph 4:17, 19). In both letters, the man or woman who has done these evil deeds has died (Col 3:3/Eph 2:1-5), although such death is understood differently by each author. In both letters, a "new humanity" has come to life, created in God's "image." In both letters, Christians are exhorted to "put on" this new humanity and so to live a new life characterized by the virtues of peace and love in place of the vice and immortality that characterizes humanity apart from Christ for both our authors (Col 3:12-15/Eph 4:31-5:7). We have only to look back to the metaphor of the church as Christ's body to realize that this "new humanity" is none other than Christ himself. As the "Paul" of Colossians says immediately, "Christ is everything in all of you" (Col 3:11, cf. Eph 1:22-23; 2:10). Again it is impossible not to notice the great resemblance in theological ideas and in their expression between these two Pauline letters.

Finally, both Colossians and Ephesians provide specific instructions for Christian moral behavior. These instructions are given in a form familiar in the ancient world and by no means exclusive to Christian literature or ethics. This form is called a *Haustafel*, or a list of household duties, and provides an ideal social model for the smooth operation of an ancient Graeco-Roman household. It can be found in Colossians 3:18-4:1 and Ephesians 5:22-6:9. In reading these texts you will notice that the selection from the Epistle to the Ephesians is much longer than that from the

Epistle to the Colossians, a stylistic tendency that we will observe repeatedly in this volume. Nevertheless you should be able to pick out a list of specific directives for the various members of a Christian household—wives (Col 3:18/Eph 5:22), husbands (Col 3:19/Eph 5:25), children (Col 3:20/Eph 6:1), fathers (Col 3:21/Eph 6:4), slaves (Col 3:22/Eph 6:5) and slave owners or masters (Col 4:1/Eph 6:9). These instructions are quite stereotyped and occur in the same order in both letters. Only where additions are made to the basic outline can we see the individual thought of the author. This is clearly the case in Colossians 3:22-25, where the author expresses a particular concern for the status and behavior of slaves in Christian community. Similarly, in Ephesians 5:22-33 the author of the letter has considerably enlarged the instructions for wives and husbands, using a common social teaching about marriage as the vehicle for expressing the unity of Christ and his church and their relationship to one another; in this process he transforms that common view of marriage as a social institution into a Christian theological category.

On three levels, then, we have seen a great deal of similarity between these two Pauline epistles—in the areas of christology, ecclesiology and ethics. Yet differences between them are almost as immediately apparent. The Epistle to the Ephesians is longer, less specific and often more sophisticated theologically. A very large proportion of the two letters is nearly identical in thought and wording in the original language, but not always in order. An attentive reader has the haunting feeling of reading the same letter, yet not the same letter—the same thought, yet not the same thought. Many scholars think that a relationship of literary dependence exists between Ephesians and Colossians,[4] although

---

[4]The book by Leander Keck and Victor Paul Furnish, *The Pauline Letters*, referenced earlier, is especially helpful in enabling the reader to see the dynamic relationship which exists between these two epistles and to understand its theological importance.

they do not always agree about which letter served as the source and which the revision. Since the Epistle to the Colossians is the shorter of the two letters, and the one more closely tied to specific events of church life, it seems most reasonable to suppose that Colossians is the earlier letter and that the author of the Epistle to the Ephesians used it as the most important, though not the only, model for the new letter within the Pauline letter tradition. That is the position that will be assumed here, and therefore we will discuss the Epistle to the Colossians first. We will become familiar with the world of Colossians, with the way in which these Christians articulated their faith in Jesus Christ in terms of the world they knew, and with the way in which they expressed their faith in daily life in that world. Then we will be able, in the following section, to see the more sophisticated Epistle to the Ephesians as the natural progression of the theological message of Paul himself through time and history. Throughout our discussion of these Pauline epistles, constant reference will be made to Paul's own letters as the source of the message about Christ that each author re-expresses in a changing world to a church with changing needs. Since as modern Christians, we are called to express the same faith in our own world and for our own churches, the efforts of these Christian "ancestors" of ours might become a model for our own efforts.

2

The Epistle to the Colossians

Introduction

Because of the doubts which surround the question of its authorship, it is difficult to describe with precision the date of the letter, the community to which Colossians was written, the events that had transpired to call forth the letter, or the society in which its author lived. The question of date must be left entirely open. If written by Paul himself, the letter would have to have been written around 58-63 C.E. If pseudonymous, as we prefer to presume here, Colossians could have been written at any time between 60-80 C.E. Regardless of this uncertainty, as we read the letter several things about the community of Christians living in Colossae emerge as particularly significant.

It is clear from Col 1:5-8 and 2:1 that, even if the Epistle to the Colossians had been written by the Apostle Paul, the community of Christians at Colossae was not founded by Paul and had never seen him in person. The Colossians had received the message of the gospel from Epaphras. Whether written by the Apostle himself or by one of his disciples in Paul's name, surely one of the purposes which the letter was intended to serve was to back up the original preaching of Epaphras in Colossae with the apostolic authority of Paul. In Col 1:7 Paul endorses Epaphras, probably from beyond the grave, as "our dear fellow slave, who represents us as a faithful minister of Christ." This is to say that the gospel that Epaphras preached was an essentially Pauline message about Christ, valid because it truly represented the teaching that Paul himself would have given if he had been present among them.

We do not have to look very far to discover why the author of the Epistle to the Colossians felt that it was necessary to invoke the authority of the great apostolic teacher in this way. Especially in one section of the letter, its author reveals that the Christian community in Colossae was a threatened community. From the warnings in Col 2:4-8 and 16-23 we can see that the Pauline gospel represented by the letter itself was not the only message about Christ that was heard in Colossae, and that the community there was in danger of abandoning its original faith and practice in favor of a different point of view and way of life. The letter reaffirms a Pauline way of understanding Jesus Christ and the meaning of his life and death both for the universe and for the individual Christian believer, but does so with the intention of refuting what its author believes to be incorrect in "another gospel" (cf. II Cor 11:4) that the Colossians must have heard. This element of refutation itself may have introduced some development into the basic Pauline presentation of the gospel message, a development that accounts for differences which we can detect today, as we read the New Testament epistles, between the thought of Paul in I Corinthians, for example, and the particular emphasis of Colossians itself.

The idea that there was considerable diversity within earliest Christianity is increasingly familiar today, both in scholarly circles as well as among the other critical readers of the New Testament. Anyone who has read Paul's own letters to the Galatians and the Corinthians carefully must be aware that Paul himself encountered serious opposition during his own lifetime.[5] There were significant differences in the way various Christian groups understood the identity of Jesus Christ as God's Son, in the way they expressed the place of Jesus' death on the cross in the plan of God, in the way they worked out the relationship between belief in Jesus and life in the world. We know that Paul was only one among a large number of Christian missionary preachers, even to the Gentiles who were his special charge (cf. Gal 1:16, 2:9; Rom 11:13). These missionaries did not all preach an identical message, although we must assume that those, at least, who are known to us from the New Testament literature did all preach a message about Jesus Christ in sincerity and with conviction. They probably differed, for the most part, not in their fundamental belief in Jesus Christ, but in the total picture into which they integrated that belief. In short, like Christians in all ages, Christians in the New Testament period differed as individuals; they differed in worldview; they differed in social and religious background. The universe of meaning in which faith in Christ is articulated can lead to quite diverse formulations of belief and action. It is just this reciprocal relationship between one's understanding of the

[5]Galatians 1:6-9; 5:1-12; 6:12-13; II Corinthians 10:7-18; 11:12-31; 12:11-19. These texts give ample evidence of the opposition Paul faced in his ministry and of the existence of divergent theological points of view. Paul's indignation against false apostles and the message they preached also tells us that not all levels of diversity were tolerable to him. The process of canonization which created the New Testament as we know it illustrates both sides of this issue. In assembling a canonical collection of books and letters which are not identical to one another in form or content, the early church chose to accept as standard a certain level of difference in the theological emphasis and interest. On the other hand, by excluding some books from that collection the early church made it clear that certain expressions of belief in Jesus Christ current at the time were nevertheless not valid ones. On the formation of the New Testament canon, see Harry V. Gamble, *The New Testament Canon*. Guides to Biblical Scholarship (Philadelphia: Fortress Press, 1985).

universe as a whole and one's spirituality as a Christian that we have set out to study in this volume on the basis of several authors in the Pauline tradition.

In Colossians, we encounter immediately a clash of world-view which has resulted in two conflicting forms of Christian spirituality. For the author of the Epistle to the Colossians the new preaching which had come to Colossae was unacceptable. The missionaries who brought this different message were false teachers, opponents of the true gospel, whose merely human preaching threatened the life of the Colossians in Christ. It is vital to try to understand what this false message preached in Colossae might have been. Any answer is very much determined by the question that has been asked, and the response of the letter to the Colossians is very much conditioned by the challenge of false doctrine. Unfortunately, we have no direct or unbiased information about what other teachers might have said in Colossae or about their motivations. We have no choice, then, but to try to reconstruct in imagination their ideas about the world, about Christ and about the life of the Christian on the basis of the stern warnings of the author of Colossians.

The question of the identity and background of the opponents in Colossae has long fascinated scholars. Although no particular group known to us from other sources from exactly this time can be certainly identified with the false teachers in Colossae, several things about them are clear enough from the letter itself. The false teachers in Colossae preached a way of being Christian that sounds quite strange to us today. According to Col 2:18 their sort of Christian life involved the "worship of angels" and Col 2:8 implies that they required service to "cosmic powers." They apparently taught and practiced a set of rules concerning eating and drinking, which made divisions between pure versus defiling activities, objects and persons, and which required participation in "yearly or monthly feasts" and sabbaths. They may even have required the Jewish ritual of circumcision (Col 2:11-13) as part of this essentially ascetic worship system. Christian life, as it was lived and taught by these opposing preachers in Colossae, necessarily involved fasting at certain times of the month or the year and probably the avoidance of certain foods altogether. We have no information now about exactly what could and could not be eaten, or about the names of their feasts and what actions were performed during their assemblies. We may suspect that many of their teachings had roots in the food laws, the rules about the "clean" and the "unclean" and the calendar of festivals and observances of the ancient Law of Moses in Judaism. But, it makes little difference today whether or not we know these things for certain. What matters for us in understanding the letter to the Colossians is what mattered to the author of the letter, that is, the *reasons* for doing whatever was done. The reasons for the way we are taught to live as Christians, at any period of Christian history, imply a fundamental understanding of the world and of the place of Christ and the Christian in that world, and this is precisely the subject of our study.

So we can say that what was *at issue* in Colossae was the way of life these early Christians should embrace because of their faith, but what was *at stake* was the way in which they understood the relationship between Jesus Christ, the universe and themselves. What can we tell, then, about the reasons for the ritual observances of these bizarre Colossian Christians which, according to the author of our epistle, threatened them with separation from God and death in a world of delusion? First of all, we would surely be correct in thinking that all of the rules to which the false teachers would have had the Colossians subject themselves had to do with their bodies and were fulfilled by disciplining the body in order to bring it into alignment with the structure of the physical universe visible, even to us, in the regular changing of the seasons and the orderly progression of the sun, moon and stars through their recurring cycles. A modern reader, educated in a scientific viewpoint so pervasive that its influence on our way of interpreting reality often goes unnoticed, understands such patterns in the physical universe as evidence of a principle of cause and effect determined by the nature of matter itself. To the ancient mind, however, such patterns were evidence of the power and activity of *personal* agents responsible for the governance of the physical universe just as each individual person is responsible for his or her own bodily actions, such as eating or fasting at regular intervals. The powers that controlled the universe were often thought to be visible in the heavenly bodies—sun, stars, and moon—which, then as now, were understood to influence the ebb and flow of the tide, the alternation of night and day, summer and winter. To the eye of the human being, earth-bound and vulnerable to the forces of nature, such "cosmic powers" must have appeared formidable indeed. It is not surprising, then, that some of the men and women in the small Christian community in Colossae would have been willing to placate and please these powers by imitation of their cyclic activities. The reason, therefore, for the variety of rituals that threatened to become part of the Christianity of Colossae was the giving of worship and honor to astral powers through the ordering of the lives of men and women in honor of daily, weekly, monthly and yearly patterns determined by those powers.

Scholars have often speculated about the exact nature and names of these "powers of the universe" and just how their influence could have entered into early Christianity, as it so obviously had. The use of the name "angels" in Col 2:18 seems to indicate Judaism as the source of the rituals and therefore the belief system that supported them, as does the mention of the sabbath in 2:16 and of circumcision in 2:11. However, the pair "principality and power" in Col 2:10 points to a Graeco-Roman intellectual environment.[6] Really, there is no contest between these two possible background environments for the type of religious thought apparently represented by the false teachers in Colossae. Belief in the powers of nature and religious observances honoring them and seeking their help are as old and widespread as is human culture itself. For our purposes in discussing the Epistle to the Colossians we need only recognize that the Christians of Colossae lived and thought in a universe that was filled with powerful beings who had a direct influence on human life. The problem confronting this small group of early Christian believers was integrating faith in Jesus Christ into this perception of reality and living an authentically Christian life in a hostile universe.

If it is clear from Col 1:13 and 2:15 that the "powers that be" are hostile to both God and humanity, it is equally clear that God has triumphed over them in Christ for the sake of Christian believers. The importance of this aspect of reality in the theology of Colossians is obvious to us because of the polemic against false teachers into which the message of the letter is set. The author of our letters does not deny the existence of cosmic powers and angels in the presentation of Christian faith. On the contrary, the author comes to terms with their existence on the basis of belief that Jesus Christ is truly the Son of God in a way that the opponents had not thought of, in a way that Paul himself had

---

[6]See Pheme Perkins, *Reading the New Testament* (New York: Paulist Press, 1978) pp. 23-61, 111-127, for a brief, readable and very helpful overview of Jewish and Graeco-Roman culture and religion in the New Testament period; also Sean Freyne, *The World of the New Testament*. New Testament Message 2. (Wilmington, DE: Michael Glazier, 1980). pp. 3-78.

not developed very much, at least not in his writings which are left to us now, although the roots of the idea lie deep beneath his thought in the Epistle to the Romans and the Corinthian letters. For the Epistle to the Colossians, Christ is the absolute ground of *all* visible reality as the image of God and the first-born of creation, as well as the crucified and resurrected Lord. Because of this dual christology, elaborated as a response to the world as experienced by the Colossian Christians, our author can reject participation in the "worship of angels" in any form for Christians who properly belong to a power far superior to any "principality" —Christ himself, and Christ alone.

The Christological Structure of Reality
According to the Epistle to the Colossians

When we read and study the Epistle to the Colossians, our subject is the universe as a whole. The Christians in Colossae were not just members of a local church or citizens of the political system created by Graeco-Roman domination of Asia Minor. They were human beings confronting reality as a cosmic totality in terms of their belief in Jesus Christ. They saw both Christ and themselves against the backdrop of the universe. Or, taking the opposite point of view, the author of Colossians used Jesus Christ as the key with which the meaning of the universe as a whole was unlocked. This is partially because of the challenge of false teachers which we have discussed, and partially because the faith of Paul himself was cosmic in scope.

The first chapter of the epistle contains a famous hymn of praise to Jesus Christ, which describes his nature and his functions in terms of the very structure of reality. Col 1:15-20 is probably a fragment of a prayer or song used by Christians of the first century in their worship and inserted into our letter because it expressed the kind of faith needed by the community in its time of crisis. The original provenance and form of this poetic fragment are unknown, so we cannot say that its christology arose solely or specifically to meet a challenge of false teaching similar to that encountered in Colossae, but neither can we doubt its relevance nor fail to see its usefulness for our author. The predominant theme of the hymn is very clear: the Christ in whom the Colossians must believe is the foundation of all existence and the primary link between the world of experience and God, as both creator and redeemer. Colossians 1:15-20 has much in common theologically with the beginning of the Gospel of John, often called the "Prologue," which is also considered to be a hymn used by early Johannine Christian communities in their worship. It is interesting to reflect on the fact that faith is often expressed in worship before it is used in arguments. The many similarities between these two hymns, stemming from quite distinct early Christian groups, attest to the rapid growth of belief in Christ as a pre-existent, divine and cosmic figure in the latter decades of the first century.

Here is the hymn, set into the form of a poem. It is not meant to reproduce the original form of the hymn, since scholars do not agree about the details of its reconstruction. Nevertheless, when you read the text as a poem, you will be able to see the parallelism used to construct it and understand more easily the fact that the hymn is centered on Christ alone and describes him in various stages of his existence and work.

> He is the image of the Invisible God
>   the first-born of all creatures.
> In him everything in heaven and on earth was created,
>   things visible and invisible,
>   whether thrones or dominations,

> principalities or powers;
>> all were created through him,
>>> and for him.
> He is before all else that is.
> In him everything continues in being.
> It is he who is head of the body,
>> the church;
> he who is the beginning,
>> the first-born from the dead,
>>> so that primacy may be his in everything.
> It pleased God to make absolute fullness reside in him and by
> means of him, to reconcile everything
> in his person,
>>>> both on earth and in the heavens,
>>> making peace by the blood of his cross.

In this study of Colossians we will use Col 1:15-20 as a beginning and pivotal point from which to explore the message of the letter as a whole. This is possible because the hymn presents in the terse yet evocative language of poetry the truth that the letter as a whole proclaims and explains. Notice the things that it says about Jesus Christ, the "beloved Son" of God (Col 1:10-13). The praises can be grouped in three categories: 1) Christ in relation to God, his Father, 2)Christ in relation to the universe and 3)Christ in relation to the church, those who believe in him. We will discuss these in order, with special attention to background information which can help us to understand the hymn as did the early Christians who prayed it, and so share more fully in their praise.

GOD AND CHRIST—COLOSSIANS 1:15

Christ stands in the closest possible relationship to God himself. "He is the image of the Invisible God." (Col 1:15). Christ is certainly divine for the author of Colossians, the visible reflection of a God who is in himself invisible. Trinitarian doctrine and ways of thinking about the nature of God, in which the term "image" is currently used, are familiar to many Christians today, so familiar that they can be taken for granted. This is the legacy of centuries of Christian thinkers who have pondered and refined our way of expressing the experience of God in Christ and Spirit. It is good to remember, however, that for Christians of the earliest centuries of the church this was a hard-won insight. At the time the letter to Colossae was written, for example, Christians were engaged in a real *effort* to grasp and convey the identity, yet distinction, that they saw between Jesus Christ and the God who had long been revealing himself to humankind through his chosen people, the Jews. For most Christians, God still revealed himself in the Scriptures of that people—the books that we call the Old Testament. The Old Testament and the new revelation of God in Christ were understood to be closely related.

The first way that the relationship between Jesus Christ and the God of the Old Testament was expressed by the earliest Christians, such as Paul himself, was with the imagery of "Father and Son." The imagery is still present and important in Colossians also. In Col 1:3 God is called "the Father of our Lord Jesus Christ," as he is by implication in Col 1:12 and 3:17. Christ Jesus himself is called the "beloved Son" in Col 1:13. Earlier Pauline letters, which are certainly Paul's own, are full of this Father/Son imagery, as are all of the gospels. It is the earliest and most fundamental way of expressing the relationship between Jesus and the God who had become known in the history of Israel. A good example to look at from Paul's own letters comes from the Epistle to the Romans. Romans 8:18-39 illustrates Paul's own use of the Father/Son description of the relationship between Christ and God as well as his extension of this imagery to refer to all Christian believers as "sons of God" (Rom 8:14, 19, 29 passim).

Chapter 8 of the Epistle to the Romans is interesting for the study of Colossians in many ways. For example, in Romans 8:38-39 Paul himself is concerned with "angels," "principalities," "height," "depth" and any "other creature" that might be seeking to separate the believing "children of God" from their loving Father. He is as confident as is the author of Colossians, against anyone who might think otherwise, that no other being, no matter how powerful or superior to human beings, is able to destroy the salvation that comes to us from God through Jesus Christ. When we read the later letters of the New Testament, it is helpful to realize that earlier answers to similar questions and problems are often the springboard for later theological develop-ments. Paul's own confidence that nothing can separate us from the love of God because we are God's adopted children comes from his conviction that, though we often suffer as Jesus did when he died on the cross, we will surely be glorified as Jesus was when God raised him from the dead, because it is God's will to choose us for salvation in his own son (Rom 8:18, 28-29, 32, 34-35 passim). God's will can overcome *any* opposition to this plan, as the resurrection of his own son testifies. We will see these same ideas reappear in the Epistle to the Ephesians. The author of the Epistle to the Colossians however, while accepting this solution, chooses to elaborate on it in another direction. While Paul's own emphasis, typically, is on salvation and resur-rection, our author's focus is on the creation of the world.

So, instead of discussing the sonship of Jesus Christ further, the "Paul" of Colossians has chosen the concept of "image" to express the nature of Christ and through him, the nature of reality. At this time, in philosophy as well as in the Old Testament, the word "image" had been associated, quite consistently with the origin, nature, or creation of the world. To use the word at all was to let one's readers know that the stage was set for a discussion of events which occurred at the very beginning of time, at the foundation of everything that has ever come to be. Even for a modern reader, to call Jesus Christ "the image of God" is a reminder of the story of the creation of the first human beings that is told in the early chapters of the Book of Genesis.

Genesis 1:27 reads "God created man in his image; in the divine image he created him; male and female he created them," and our author has something quite similar in mind in Col 1:15-17. In Genesis we are told that humankind, male and female, was created by God. This creation, however, was accomplished "in his [God's] image." This is a difficult phrase and a confusing one. It could be interpreted in several ways. It could mean, for example, that the first man and woman were created according to a kind of divine pattern—God's "Image." Or, it could mean that they were created as two parts of a whole, itself an image of the deity. In either case, God's image would be considered to be a concrete reality, divine yet somehow distinct from God. Or, it could simply mean that men and women *resemble* God. In this case, the "image of God" would be humanity itself. As you can see, this text could easily be susceptible to *mis*interpretation. This is true to such an extent that within Judaism of the early centuries of our era only the most skilled interpreters of the scriptures were allowed to discuss Genesis 1:26-27 at all, and even they were discouraged from doing so. Nevertheless both Jewish and Christian thinkers were busily doing just that—speculating on the meaning of this ambiguous phrase that held the secret to the beginnings of human existence.

In using the very evocative word "image" to refer to Jesus Christ, the beloved Son of God, the author of Colossians is revealing knowledge of and participation in such speculation.

In the common philosophical speech of those times, "image" meant "reflection," just as it does now. We should think of a reflection in a mirror or a painted or sculpted representation of something else. With the advent of modern photographic and electronic duplicating techniques, not to mention machine-made glass mirrors, we have come today to think of an image as a potentially perfect or near perfect reproduction of its original. Even for us, however, a copy is never quite as good as the original. In the ancient world, where mirrors were polished metal and copy techniques consisted of artistic representation, an image was understood to be an inferior reality. An image had a share in the very essence of its original but it was reduced and derivative reality.

If you have studied ancient philosophy, you know that the thought of Plato is the philosophical system in which the word "image" is the most at home.[7] Platonic philosophy was among the most pervasive ways of understanding reality in the first century, so popular that it had become considerably watered down and its categories used almost unconsciously as the common coin of speaking and writing. Many street-corner philosophers taught a kind of popular Platonism in which the structure of reality itself was understood to be a series of "images" descending in order from the realm of the divine—one image derived from another, sometimes in pairs—until the world as we see and experience it came to be as a very inferior copy of the divine

[7]Perkins, *Reading the New Testament* pp. 120-121; *The Dictionary of Bible and Religion*, ed. William H. Gentz (Nashville: Abingdon Press, 1986) "Plato/Platonism," pp. 822-823.

world from which it ultimately flows. The farther removed from the original reality, however, the less "real" the image. Within such a popular Platonic system, the astral bodies, for example, would be images of the divine world of a higher order than those found on earth—of a more "spiritual" and less "physical" type, much more powerful, and more alive. As you remember, it is just such cosmic beings and their relationship to Jesus Christ and to Christian believers that our author is concerned with in writing Colossians.

Here we have, then, the three parts of the background that will ultimately explain the hymn in praise of Jesus Christ that we have read in Colossians 1:15-20—the Pauline theology of the Christ who died on the cross and was raised up for the salvation of those who believe in him, the Old Testament story of the creation of the world and humankind, and popular philosophical categories of the time. Out of these elements the Christian author of Colossians has created a synthesis of meaning in which faith in Christ is integrated with the basic comprehension of the world that was a common cultural and religious heritage. Out of this synthesis a universe of meaning emerges that is authentically and uniquely Christian. We will use this tripartite background throughout our study of Colossians and Ephesians to explain the texts and fill them with meaning for ourselves as they were full of meaning for their original readers. Only in this way can we hope to create for ourselves a faith and a spirituality that is authentically biblical. Once understanding the faith of our author, we can begin to form a dynamic contemporary expression of it in response to our own needs. In this process the Epistle to the Colossians is a springboard for our own reflections, in somewhat the same way that the preaching and letters of Paul were for the writer of Colossians. We have already begun to discuss the nature of Christ's relationship to God according to Colossians

1:15. With the help of the background presented so briefly here, we can deepen our appreciation of it and show the connection with what follows—Christ's relationship to the world—much more clearly. When our author says in Col 1:15 that Christ is "the image of the Invisible God," the scriptural and philosophical backgrounds are especially important.

Within Judaism God had been revealed in historical events and in the written word of scripture, but he had been revealed to be not only a God who entered into human lives and the events of human history but, even more, to be a God who was mysterious, totally transcending human categories of understanding, not immanent in the world but increasingly aloof from it. This was a refinement of the idea of God. It stood in sharp contrast to what we ordinarily think of when we think of the paganism of the first century—for example, the Greek and Roman gods and goddesses with their all-too-human quarrels, rages and interference in human affairs. However, it left the Judaism of the time with a deep-rooted need to experience God, though he be invisible and beyond human understanding, a need Judaism shared with its pagan neighbors. It also resulted in an experience of the precariousness of life in the world, far-removed from the God to be followed and loved, the God from whom rescue had come in the past—in the exodus from Egypt and the return from exile in Babylon. God had seemed so close to his people then, but in the centuries immediately before the Christian era, God sometimes seemed very far away indeed, and the world a very friendly place for Jews and pagans alike. It is easy for us to understand the need to experience God that these people felt so long ago, because we feel it too. Every one of us has at some time in our lives felt the longing for God to reach out in help or comfort in times of pain, just as we reach out to God in sorrow and in joy. And we have no need to be told about the

precariousness of our existence—we read about it every day
in our newspapers and can feel the full force of the dangers we
face as we sit in our own homes and watch scenes of violence
on television.

As the "image" of the invisible and transcendent God, Jesus
Christ made the inaccessible God suddenly and miraculously
accessible—in the world instead of far away, very *recently* and not
in the "long ago" of biblical history. As image Christ shares in the
divine nature, because in the philosophy of the time, an image
had a share in the reality of the original. As image, also because of
the meaning the concept had at the time, Christ was a slightly
different reality, a reality one step closer to our experience. The
Father is invisible, but the beloved Son, as image, is visible. The
Christ of Colossians is God himself in visible form, although God
himself is not visible. Today it is still Christ's function to make
God present to the world. Christ is still God touching our lives
and holding our world together, however much it seems to be
tearing itself apart. We have much to learn from Colossians about
how and why he is able to do this.

In biblical history, the most important way in which God had
become visible to those who believed in him and followed his
ways was in his actions on their behalf. The most important of
God's actions for the benefit of humanity was creation itself. The
very use of the word "image" would suggest to the ancient reader
within the religious heritage of Judaism, as all Christians ultimately
are, that creation was bound to come up as a topic in the
discussion. It appears immediately, at the end of Col 1:15. Christ's
relationship to God as image is only given one-half of a verse, but
his relationship to God's creation is given a full two and one-half
verses, Col 1:15b-17.

CHRIST AND THE UNIVERSE—COLOSSIANS 1:15b-17

It is equally important, in understanding who God's Son is, to know that he is the image of his Father and to know that he is the fountainhead of all the rest of creation. We could ask how our author knows this, and we would have to answer that there is no way to get an absolute answer. Nevertheless, thinking back to the story of the creation of man and woman in Genesis 1:26-27 does suggest a possible answer. There, at the very beginning of our story, as God fashioned the world as a place for Adam and Eve and all their numberless descendants to live (cf. Gen 1:28-30), the image of God was already present and active. When humanity itself comes to be, God's image already is. In fact, the creation of man and woman takes place *in* that image. God's image, according to the story, has had a part to play in the world from the very beginning. Since the image is *God's* and does not belong to the world nor to humanity, it is reasonable to suppose that it *was* before the light, before the seas, before the heavens, indeed before anything at all that was not God came into being. If this image had a special role in the creation of man and woman, it may also have had an actual part in creating those other things—the heavens, the sun, moon and stars, the waters and the land with all their "living creatures"—that had come before to set the stage for the arrival of *human* beings.

Admittedly, we are condensing a great deal of reflection that took place over centuries of time before the Epistle to the Colossians was written into only a few pages. Yet, the Epistle to the Colossians no less than the rest of the *New* Testament stands at the end of a very, very long history of God's revelation that we call the *Old* Testament. So it should not be surprising that sometimes the new cannot really be understood without the "Old" that came before and came *along*. It is so with the paean of praise in Colossians 1:15-17. Our author begins with some understanding of the role of Christ as the divine image active in the creation of the universe, such as we have briefly outlined here, then goes on to expand this theology in a direction that will show the folly and the error of giving worship to any *inferior* "image" or power.

According to Col 1:16-17 Christ as the image of God is the origin, the agent and the goal of *all* of creation. Christ is "before all else that is" both in time and in stature. He is the one being through whom *everything* else that we see or know about comes into existence. The whole universe, from the angelic powers in the heavens to the things of the earth, exists only for his sake. The world as we see or know about it continues to exist only through his power to keep it so. Like a huge invisible net, the being of Christ encompasses all other things and keeps them in place. He is the pattern for everything else, and everything, from the greatest of the heavenly powers to the lowliest earthly creature, possesses a part of his own reality. This is the way that the author of the Epistle to the Colossians understands the structure of reality. The universe is essentially "christological," that is, informed and secured by the very nature of Christ himself, and through him, by the nature of the "Invisible God." This is God's plan for his own self-revelation. The power and the wisdom of God are only fully revealed in Christ (cf. Col 1:19;2:2-3).

It is clearly foolish and contrary to the divine will, therefore, to offer reverence and worship to anyone or anything other than Christ, and through him, to God. It is probably true that, along with other thinkers of the time, the author of Colossians believed that spiritual powers— whether they be called "thrones," "principalities" or "angels"—were themselves "images" of a sort, true creatures of God and partial reflections of his power and his goodness. Only in Christ, however, is the *fullness* of God present and visible.

We have received this understanding of Christ and his relationship to God the Father and to the whole of created reality
as the legacy of our ancestors in faith. As true and faithful
followers of Christ and the teaching of the Apostle Paul about
Christ, the Christians in the small city of Colossae, on the banks
of a river in what is now modern Turkey, were called to believe
that their entire universe was held securely in the hand of God
through his visible representation, Jesus Christ. These early Christians had an understanding of the phyical structure of the universe
that we would find hard to share today. They believed that the
skies were filled with powerful superhuman beings, able to influence human events for good or for evil. We believe that the
stars and the planets are lifeless matter, moving according to
energy forces which are as impersonal as they are unconcerned
with our lives and our destiny on earth. Apart from our religious
heritage, we might see no purpose in the design of the universe,
while they saw the creation of the world itself as directed toward
the self-revelation of God in Christ. For us, the earth is an
insignificant planet in a minor solar system, created by distant
forces almost completely unknown to us. For them, the earth,
although dark, humble and admittedly far from the brilliant and
ethereal heavenly places, still was the center of created reality
because it was on earth that God chose to fully reveal himself to
his whole creation in Jesus Christ.

These differences between our perception of reality and the
meaning that we find in the universe which we inhabit, and
those of the Epistle to the Colossians are vast. Yet, upon reflection,
we can see that they do not prevent us from understanding and
even identifying with the witness of Colossians to faith and life in
Christ. For example, the Colossian Christians felt threatened by
the universe in which they lived, by malicious angels or demi-
gods visible in the skies at night. Most modern Christians, if they
are thoughtful and consider the dangers on earth and in the stars

today, have good reason to be threatened also. We may not be tempted to personify and worship the forces of nature instead of the power of God. But, threatened and frightened we certainly are. The danger now comes from within ourselves, from the technological power we have developed over the very same physical universe that the Colossians saw as semi-divine, from the inability of our societies to preserve rather than to destroy life at every level. We are tempted to worship not angels, but ourselves, instead of God. So, even though our world is perceived quite differently, we are not such different Christians from the few early believers who received this letter originally. Because it is part of the New Testament, we are, in a sense, still receiving the Epistle to the Colossians today. We are still asked to believe that Jesus Christ is the revelation of the fullness of God. Most importantly, we are called by Colossians to believe that he holds the universe together, that everything we see exists for his sake alone, that the power of God safeguards our world and ourselves through Jesus Christ. We are called to worship him alone. We are challenged not to fear, because God is at the very heart of the world through Christ and so we are not alone or abandoned. This should not lead to a naive over-confidence, but to hope, to a respect for our world and to care for it as God's possession and Christ's domain.

These are difficult things to believe and to do. The simple statements of the epistle do not *prove* to us today that they are true, but call us to faith. It was probably just as difficult for the first readers of this Pauline letter to believe its message. They were quite as serious about their own knowledge of the universe as we are about ours. The author warns them, and us, against the seduction of human reasoning which stands against the wisdom and knowledge of God revealed in Jesus Christ. Reread these warnings in Colossians 2:4-8, 16-18, 20-23. Try to imagine that *modern* physics and astronomy are the "merely human traditions and doctrines" that the author has in mind. If you can do this, you will begin to understand the challenge that this letter was to the Christians in Colossase. They were asked to look at the entire cosmos from the point of view of faith in Jesus Christ. I think we can assume that they were as convinced that there were powers in the universe that needed to be placated as we are that there are forces in the universe that are beyond control. Yet we as Christians are all called upon to believe that the world as we know it has its origin and its destiny in Christ alone. We are asked to walk in a world under God's contol. We are asked to live in a world shaped by Jesus Christ.

CHRIST AND THE CHURCH—COLOSSIANS 1:18-20

As believers, the Christians in Colossae had an even closer relationship to Christ than simply being part of the vast universe dependent upon him for its nature, its structure and its continued existence. Christians, called together into a unity under Christ as the head (Col 1:18), are the center of a universe being renewed by God. This new world is begun in the church as Christ's body. The new body of Christ is created and grows (2:19) as the world in general, and humankind in particular, is reconciled to God through the death of Christ on the cross (1:30). The participation of Christians in that suffering in the world (1:24) is witness to the continuing reconciliation in Christ and the triumph of God (2:14-15).

The world of the Colossians, although "Christ-shaped" in its very beginnings, was in the process of a vast overhaul. God in Jesus Christ was reshaping creation into close correspondence

with his own image. In the aeons of time before the birth, death
and resurrection of Jesus Christ, the world had somehow become
inimical to its creator and therefore perverted in its own nature.
The Colossian Christians too had been alienated from God and
rooted instead in evil deeds of every kind (1:21; 3:7). Where
there should have been life created by God, there was death
caused by sin. By receiving the gospel, accepting it and placing
their hope in Christ, the Colossian Christians began to participate
in a process of restoration intended by God to recreate each of
them in his own image, that is, Christ. Together the Christians at
Colossae, indeed all Christians everywhere in all times, are called
to form a single perfect person, Christ himself. In Jesus Christ,
our author states very clearly twice in the course of this brief
letter (Col 1:19; 2:9), that God had freely and lovingly chosen to
dwell in bodily form. This means not only that the fullness of
God was present on earth in Jesus Christ, the human person, but
also that the fullness of God dwells in that perfect person, the
Christ, whose body is the church in heaven and on earth.
Through the church, God himself is pleased to fill the world
which he created.

In order to understand more fully this self-identity to which
the Epistle to the Colossians calls its threatened little congregation, some more background information will be helpful. As
modern readers we are not as familiar with the philosophical and
theological presuppositions of the ancient writers of the New
Testament as we should be. Although we can see the main
contours of the Colossians' understanding of themselves, and we
can repeat their words, sometimes they can be empty words for
us unless we can fill them with meaning. The work of scholars
on the history and literature of the New Testament period can
provide the "filling" for the idea of the cosmic body of Christ, for
example, and allow us to get in touch with what the author

meant by using it.

In the most popular philosophical movement of this period of history, called Stoicism,[8] the universe was considered to be a single organism—a body—with a single rational spirit which gave it life and order. In this philosophy, all things were seen as parts of a whole. Everything affected everything else; nothing was random or isolated. This cosmic "body" was locked into an eternal cycle of birth, growth, and eventual decline and destruction, only to begin its life again and again. Not all parts of this Stoic world view are relevant to the Epistle to the Colossians, nor congenial to the development of Christian faith. For example, in biblical thought the course of history is *linear*, not cyclic. Time has a definite beginning and a single end. However, many scholars think that the Stoic idea of the *organic* nature of reality was one very important element in the original use of the metaphor of the "body of Christ" to refer to the Christian church in Corinth by the Apostle Paul himself.

I Corinthians 12:12-27 is Paul's own description of what it means for the church to be Christ's body. It would be helpful if you would read this text now to see how Paul uses the idea. There are clearly some resemblances between Paul's view of the church and the Stoic view of the world. The church is a christological microcosm. It is an organic reality, living with a single spirit (I Cor 12:12-13). Though made up of diverse parts (I Cor 12:14ff.), the good of the whole body is of primary importance, not the good of any single part (I Cor 12:25-26). All must work together and what happens to one part happens to all. As a whole, the body which is the church is identified with Christ (I Cor 12:27). This degree of humanization and the particular

[8]Perkins, *Reading the New Testament* pp. 121-122; *The Interpreter's Dictionary of the Bible*, volume 4, ed. G. A. Burtrick (Nashville: Abingdon Press, 1962) pp. 443-445.

personal identification of the ecclesiological organism is a distinctive feature of Paul's use of the concept. Moreover, two additional differences exist as well between the commonly used Stoic idea and the Pauline theological concept. There is no trace in Paul of the Stoic idea of the cyclic birth and destruction of this organic world. The body of Christ for Paul is destined for eternal glory in heaven with God (I Cor 15:22-28, 49-53). Furthermore, the words "organic world" are not really applicable to Paul's use of the expression, since he refers to a local congregation of Christians and not to a cosmic reality.

Paul's goal is a pragmatic one. Although he does say that as a group the Christian believers in Corinth have been baptized "into one body" (I Cor 12:13) and that body is Christ's body (I Cor 12:27), his aim in saying so is ethical instruction, just as Stoicism was primarily a moral philosophy. Paul wants to provide a ground for his argument that there is no reason for rivalry or division within the church of Christ. All Christians live in a unity as indivisible as a human body or as Christ himself, and in this unity each individual Christian is equal in identification with Christ. The source of this unity is the possession of a *single spirit*—God's spirit—by each baptized and believing Christian.

The use of the idea of the body of Christ to express the nature of the church in the Epistle to the Colossians is related both to the Stoic background and the practical theology of Paul. In fact, Colossians seems to have developed Paul's idea in the direction of its original relationship to Stoic philosophy. Recall that the stage set for the message of Colossians is the universe itself. The church as the body of which Christ himself is the head must have cosmic dimensions, because the Christ of Colossians has cosmic functions. In Colossians, therefore, the Christian believers are part of a body of universal proportions. The Christ of which these ancient believers have become parts is of such stature as to rival and even exceed the astral powers or universal spirits in power. Remember that the fullness of God himself dwells within him.

The Christians in Colossae, therefore, know that they are safe from any threat or danger from these powers because of their unity with Christ who has triumphed over them (Col 2:15). Even in a world full of danger these Christians were called to believe in a triumph not visible to their senses but revealed in the gospel concerning Jesus Christ preached by Epaphras. By announcing the victory of Jesus Christ over sin and death in his own death and resurrection and the forgiveness and freedom offered to men and women by a gracious and powerful God, the gospel offers the hope of life with Christ to all who hear and understand it. It offers a life free from bondage, sin and despair, not to the eyes, but to the mind and heart of all Christians.

This hope is a present reality precisely because of the identification of the Christian church as Christ's body. To each one believing in Christ, accepting the gospel and allowing it to bear fruit in daily life, is offered an intimate share in the reality of Christ himself. The author of Colossians clearly means to say that what happens to Christ happens to us also, as Christians, just as Paul says in I Corinthians 12:26, "If one member suffers, all the members suffer with it; if one member is honored, all the members share its joy." Within the universal framework of the argument of Colossians, what does this mean? It means that if Christ has died, the one who believes in him has also died (Col 3:3). It means that if Christ has been raised from the dead and now lives a new life with God in heaven, the Christian also has been raised up with Christ (Col 3:1) and lives a new life in him (Col 2:12; 3:3). This new life is not visible, just as Christ himself is not visible now. Yet it is real. The Colossians know this. Indeed it has been announced to "every creature under heaven" (Col 1:23). But the full revelation of this new life remains a hope.

After all, these early Christians lived on earth. They encountered and struggled with the realities of ordinary life just as we do. That is why hope is mentioned so frequently in the early part of this letter (see Col 1:4, 23, 27-28). In fact, the author does not let us forget the first half of Paul's summary in I Corinthians 12:26, "If one member suffers, all the members suffer with it . . . . " If Christ has suffered in his body in the act of reconciling the whole world to God, then the believer also suffers with him. Paul himself, as he is presented in Colossians, is a model for the joyful participation of the Christian in the bodily sufferings of Christ (Col 1:24).

In summary, then, we can see that the author of Colossians sees the identity of the Christian in terms of the person and actions of Jesus Christ and defines a place in the universal structure of reality for believers in terms of identification with Christ. As a member of Christ's body, the Colossian Christian is secure in a threatening world. Salvation lives and grows within the church as long as it remains in contact with Christ as "head."

The idea of the "headship" of Christ over the church, his body, is a contribution of the Pauline author of the Epistle to the Colossians to the metaphor of the body of Christ. Paul himself does not talk specifically about Christ as head of the church, or as distinct in any way from the church as his body. In fact, Paul's main point in I Corinthians was that there are *no* distinctions of dignity within the body of Christ. We may presume that Paul himself did see Christ as Lord of his Church because it is to him that all Christian believers belong as members. Paul does speak of Christ as the "head" of every man in I Corinthians 11:3, so we can be sure that Paul is the source of the idea of Christ's "headship" even if he has not used the idea in relation to the body of Christ metaphor.

To be the "head" can mean two things. First, it could mean

that, as the head, Christ is in authority over the church, just as the head of a nation, an army, a family or a committee is the person in charge. Second, it could mean that Christ is the *origin* of the church, the first and founding member, just as the head-waters of a great river are its source. Both of these possible meanings are of great importance for the author of our epistle. It is not surprising that Colossians has used the synthesis of Paul's ideas that appears in the hymn in verse 18. The ideas of supremacy in being and supremacy in power and authority are very important for our author and for the Christians in Colossae. They believe in a Christ who is before all things in time as the source of their very existence and who is above all things in space as the power which holds them in being. This faith overcomes the danger of false teaching which would have them worship the creatures of the heavens instead of Christ and through him, the Invisible God. It is this powerful Christ to whom they are connected as members of the church. The church itself grows stronger day by day through its steadfast connection to him (Col 2:19). Each individual believer is made more and more perfect (1:28; 3:10-11) as each one is recreated in the image of God through closer and closer unity with Christ.

Another element of background, this time theological rather than philosophical, will be helpful in fully appreciating the image of re-creation and renewal that is so strong in our author's understanding of the nature of Christ and the life and destiny of the Christian. The "Paul" of Colossians is very sure that something had indeed gone awry in the world that God had long ago created in and through Christ. The world of the Colossian Christians' everyday experience was one in which the image of the invisible God had dissolved in a mirror of hostility and evil. Their unity with Christ was both their hope for an everlasting future and the deepest level of their existence as Christians. But, this hope had to be lived through in a world alien to God and Christ, and to the Colossian Christians themselves.

The biblical tradition of Judaism which lies at the foundation of Christian faith contains a story of the origin of this alienation in humanity itself. The disobedience of the first human being created according to God's image, Adam, allowed the entrance of evil into the world created good by God and began the disorder and hostility which only Jesus' death on the cross could bring to an end. In the Judaeo-Christian religious tradition, the world has always been considered the work of God and as a result good. It would be helpful for you to read Genesis, Chapters 1-3, in order to recall the stories which have communicated this tradition about the origin and nature of the world to centuries of Jewish and Christian believers. For example, the same astral bodies, of which the Christians in Colossae were apparently so afraid, were fashioned by God to do his will, according to Genesis 1:14-19.

> Then God said, "Let there be lights in the dome of the sky, to separate day from night. Let them mark the fixed times, the days and the years and serve as luminaries in the dome of the sky, to shed light upon the earth." (Gen 1:14-15)

Yet it seems that by the time our letter to the church in Colossae was written by one of those who were associated with Paul in his mission, these very lights in the sky had become a barrier between humankind and its God rather than servants of God who brought light and order into the life of the world.

The scriptures are very nearly unanimous in assigning the blame for this to humanity itself. As all men and women throughout history are represented in the first human pair, created directly by God's hand, so all evil to be experienced between birth and death by their descendants is traced backed to Adam and Eve. This is so because Adam was intended by God to be his own representative on earth, to rule all things as God's viceroy. We can see this clearly in Genesis 1:28—"God blessed them, saying: 'Be fertile and multiply; fill the earth and subdue it. Have dominion over the fish of the sea, the birds of the air, and all the living things that move on the earth.'" We can see this idea again in Genesis 2:19-23 when Adam gives names to all other creatures. Adam himself had only one Lord, God, who gave him only a single commandment which expressed Adam's subjection to him as the divine Lord of the earth. In Genesis 2:16-17 Adam receives the single command of the Lord not to eat the fruit of only one tree among the myriad fruits of the garden in which he was settled and for which he was intended to care. The punishment for disobedience was to be death, since the commandment expressed his submission to God as the source of all life.

We are all familiar with the sad story of Adam and Eve's fall into disobedience, and thus into death, that is told in Genesis 3. Possibly we have never looked closely at the consequences for the world that result immediately from the eating of the fruit of the forbidden tree according to the story. The world itself becomes disorded. Enmity, hostility and domination arise, where once peace and harmony had been the rule. This is the case between man and wife (Gen 3:16), between animals and the human persons who were intended to rule them (Gen 3:15), and between the earth itself and the people who inhabit it (Gen 3:17-19). The earth becomes Adam's grave rather than his garden. Relationships between persons become characterized by violence and hostility. The story of the murder of Abel by his brother Cain told in Genesis 4 becomes typical of the lack of understanding alienation and open warfare that has been the story of a human race separated from its God ever since.

The Old Testament itself has very little to say about the effects of this hostility and disorder on the rest of visible creation beyond and above the earth, in the heavens. One could wonder, however, what effect the disorder on earth might have had on those beings superior in power and glory to human beings. Although the biblical tradition itself contains no answer, people living around the beginning of the Christian era had a special interest in this question and produced a considerable body of literature which records the answers that they gave. This literature is not included in our Bible, yet the ideas contained in it were often very important for the authors of the New Testament and express the influential ideas of the time quite clearly.[9] One of the ideas of the time which emerges very strongly in several of the books which were read widely at the time by Christians, among them Paul himself, was that the fall of Adam was connected with, and in part a result of, a revolt on the part of the angelic powers. Even today, especially for those educated in the earlier decades of our century, the story of Lucifer's refusal to worship the first human being or pre-existent Christ and his resulting fall from heaven is often more familiar than the biblical stories themselves and is frequently considered to be part of the Bible, although it is not. The idea of a revolt of the angels, or astral powers, was certainly a very popular one in the oral tradition of Judaism and other religious groups of the time, and does surface in the non-canonical literature produced at about the same time as the Epistle to the Colossians. The envy of the serpent in the biblical story of Adam and Eve is a very early and subdued form

---

[9]*Dictionary of Bible and Religion*, "Apocrypha," pp. 57-58; "Pseudepigrapha," pp. 853-854. There is an older collection of these books in translation edited by R. H. Charles, *The Apocrypha and Pseudepigrapha of the Old Testament*, Two Volumes (Oxford: At the Clarendon Press, 1913) which is available in many major libraries, and a new edition edited by James H. Charlesworth, *The Old Testament Pseudepigrapha*, Two Volumes (Garden City, New York: Doubleday & Company, Inc. 1983/1985) now in print.

of it. The serpent seems determined to usurp the authority over the earth given to Adam because of envy that such a frail and easily deceived creature could have been given such glory by his creator.

It seems quite likely that there is some such background which forms part of the world-view of the Colossian Christians. They see the astral, or angelic, powers as not only superior to themselves, but as inimical to themselves and to God. They see them as envious, desirous of worship for themselves that should in fact go to Jesus Christ and through him to God. Like the serpent in the temptation of Eve, the cosmic powers still tempt humankind to follow the creature rather than the creator.

When we read in Colossians 1:13 that Christ "rescued us from the power of darkness" and in Colossians 1:21 that the Christians "were once alienated" and "nourished hostility in your hearts because of your evil deeds," we can see the influence of this background. When Adam sinned, he lost the control of the world given to him by his creator. In a way, even according to the biblical story, you could say that Adam came to be under the power of the serpent, whose wishes he followed instead of God's. All men and women are born into the same situation of domination by evil forces beyond their control. Their actions in obedience to such dominating and enslaving evil are themselves sinful, just as Adam's and Eve's were. In the world-view of Judaism, this is especially true of Gentiles. In the case of the chosen people, the Jews, God had been continually trying to rescue his creation from the stifling grip of evil and restore it to life and goodness. He had even given the Law of Moses as a guide and a help, allowing his own people to live lives more closely resembling the lives intended for them. But the Gentiles were abandoned to the powers of evil. In the view of the Judaism of the time, their worship of astral deities was evidence of this. It is important to remember that the Christians in Colossae were most probably Gentiles (Col 1:28). In coming to faith in Jesus Christ as God's Son, they came into contact also with this view of reality and history and came to understand themselves as those "who were once alienated" from God. They came to interpret their former way of life as sinful and idolatrous. They understood that only in Christ were they rescued from the power of evil (Col 1:13), only in Christ were their former sinful deeds forgiven (Col 1:14; 2:13), only in Christ were they given life in place of the death which was their heritage from Adam and Cain, their fathers in sin (Col 2:13), and only in Christ could they freely appear before God as holy and sinless (Col 1:22). This is nothing less than a "new creation." The *many* who were sinful are renewed and reunited into the *one* who is not.

Now we can understand what our author means in writing "what you have done is put aside your old self with its past deeds and put on a new man, one who grows in knowledge as he is formed anew in the image of his Creator" (Col 3:9b-10). Just as there was unity in humankind before Christ in Adam, there is unity of humankind in Christ. In Adam destruction, death and domination by the powers of evil were the effects of sin. Through sin the image of God, according to which humankind and the world were originally created, became marred beyond recognition in the mirror of the world as we know and experience it. In Christ, on the contrary, each man and woman is re-created in the image of God until the world comes to shine in its glorious resemblance to God himself. Through their unity with the one perfect human being in whom the "fullness of deity resides in bodily form" (Col 2:9), Christians attain the perfection of the original creation (Col 1:28). To return to the worship of the powers of the universe would be to negate the work of Christ and to repeat the sin of Adam. To be united to Christ in sinlessness and peace is to eventually transform the world itself, as goodness and order gradually become the norm.

There is no doubt that the Apostle Paul himself is the source for this world-view and this particular understanding of the work of Christ in relation to the church. Rereading the Epistle to the Romans we can encounter most of these ideas. For example, in Romans 6:3-23 Paul discusses the former status of those who now believe in Christ. It was characterized by enslavement to the power of evil, typically called "Sin" by Paul himself. The wages paid by sin to its servants are very poor: death. But Christ gives life freely to those who serve God. In Romans 5:12-19 and 8:14-23 Paul makes it clear that he looks at salvation in Christ from the point of view of creation. Through sin, creation was subjected to the power of evil and shares the lot of humankind. For Paul, the world itself suffers and groans with the men and women who were intended to cultivate it. Nevertheless, because of the death of Christ on our behalf, we are destined to share the image of God's son (Rom 8:29). It seems clear, finally, that angelic, astral powers also play a part in Paul's own thought. Because of Jesus Christ, we are conquerors, in spite of suffering and trial. Paul is certain

> that neither death nor life, neither angels nor principalities, neither the present nor the future, nor powers, neither height nor depth nor any other creature, will be able to separate us from the love of God that comes to us in Christ Jesus, our Lord (Rom 8:38-39).

While he does not dwell on the subject of spiritual powers inimical to humanity, it is clear that for Paul such powers existed and posed some threat to the salvation of Christian believers. Although Paul believes that threat to be overcome in principle by Jesus Christ, the author of Colossians has seen the threat re-emerge as his community stands on the verge of worshiping powers. This worship would negate the victory of Christ won for all who believed in him over the "powers that be" in the universe. This victory was won through his death on the cross (Rom 8:3, 32; 5:6, 9-10; 6:6-10; cf. Col 1:20, 22; 2:14-15).

Living the Reality of Christ—The Call of Colossians

THE CHURCH AND THE WORLD

This is the understanding of reality—indeed this is the self-understanding—of the Christians to whom our letter was written, expressed in summary form in the hymn which has been our focal-point in Colossians so far. The world-view we have seen in the hymn permeates the letter as a whole and gives the message of Colossians its distinctive shape. Consequences flow from it for the life these Christians were called to live in Christ. The Christians who lived in the town of Colossae did not live in a world that had been *visibly* transformed by Christ. On the contrary, as they came together as believers, *they* had been transformed by Christ, and it was their task to recreate the world itself in their personal lives, in their families and in their community.

Since Christ's victory over the powers of evil had been accomplished in his cross and through his death, the Colossians' lives might also involve suffering in imitation of him. The disciple who speaks in Paul's name in Colossians holds him up as a model of willing and joyful suffering in Col 1:24, "Even now I find my joy in the suffering I endure for you. In my own flesh I fill up what is lacking in the suffering of Christ for the sake of his body, the church." For this Paul, his struggle to teach and exhort each man and woman to perfection in Christ is more God's work than his own. He says in Col 1:29, "For this I work and struggle, impelled by that energy of his which is so powerful a force within me." Whether we read "his" to mean Christ's or God's energy, it remains true that these early Christians felt that their lives were lived in God's own power and their struggle to transform the world through the power of good was in fact the activity of God himself and Christ, his image, beginning the process of creation once again through the church. In their little church, in their families, and even in their individual lives and experience, God was active in the world again, bringing it back to its original reflection of his own being. Such re-creation is truly the resurrection of the world itself from the dead.

The cosmic resurrection was begun by God in raising Christ himself (Col 1:18). Each Christian, however, sharing in the death of Jesus Christ in baptism when entering the Christian community, shares also in Christ's resurrection. For the "Paul" of Colossians it is clear that each and every one who believes in Jesus Christ is raised with him in that faith. The statement in Col 2:12 could hardly be more clear—"In baptism you were not only buried with him but also raised to life with him because you believed in the power of God who raised him from the dead." The Paul of the earlier letters, the Epistle to the Romans or the First Epistle to the Corinthians for example, is not usually willing to go quite this far when he talks about the life of those who believe in Christ in the world. In Romans 6:3-5, Paul himself asserts that Christians share in Christ's death in baptism.

> Are you not aware that we who were baptized into Christ Jesus were baptized into his death? Through baptism into his death we were buried with him, so that, just as Christ was raised from the dead by the glory of the Father, we too might live a new life. If we have been united with him through likeness to his death, so shall we be through a like resurrection.

The Apostle Paul as he writes in Romans is certainly the source for the thought of the "Paul" of Colossians. For both of them, the participation of each Christian in Christ's death is *real*. Christians have in fact died. This death is symbolized and enacted for both of them through the ritual immersion in the waters of baptism. Though living in the same *world*, Pauline Christians are not living the same *life*. Although the Apostle Paul believes that all who are baptized live a new life—Christ's life rather than their own—he does not say that they are resurrected. For Paul, a resurrection like Christ's is a *hope* for the individual believer, albeit a hope that cannot fail (Rom 6:8; 8:24-25, 29-39). For Paul, personal resurrection necessarily involves the death and/or transformation of the physical body (I Cor 15:12-55). This will happen only when the world as we know it has come to an end.

The "Paul" of Colossians says something a bit different. For him the resurrection of the Christian has already taken place (Col 3:1). It is, perhaps, simply a more literal reading of the Apostle Paul's statement that we all possess a new life in Christ. The author of the Epistle to the Colossians certainly knows that this little congregation is not living in heaven! Their bodies have undergone neither death nor transformation. They still have families, positions in society to maintain, and temptations aplenty. They still can look up at the same stars and be tempted to worship them as gods, or demi-gods. Nevertheless, we can say that they have been raised with Christ and live a new life. The author expresses this paradox by saying that their new life is "hidden now with Christ in God." The transformation of each Christian is real and complete; it needs only to be *revealed*, in God's own time.

Like most Christians of the first century, indeed most Christians today, our author knew where Christ, and so the hidden life of each believer, was to be found. Christ is seated at the right hand of God as a divine and exalted king, to return at the appointed time to judge the world and all its inhabitants (Mk 13:26-27; Lk 24:50-51; I Thess 4:16-17; I Cor 15:24-25; Col 3:1; cf. Psalm 110 and Daniel 7). So we are left with a strange tension in Colossians concerning the nature of Christian life. Christians are on the earth, but their true life is in the highest heaven—far above the visible heavens which seemed so alive and so threatening to the Colossians—with the true God. The letter urges all Christians, therefore, to fix their minds and set their hearts on the "higher realms" where Christ and their very selves sit hidden from their eyes.

More than this, the "Paul" of Colossians calls upon all Christians to *live out* this glorious but invisible life in this world. To do so will be to infuse the earth with the very life of God. Christians must cast aside behavior that is characteristic of humanity of old (Col 3:5-11), a sinful humanity, deserving of God's wrath and punishment, a divided and hostile humanity, no longer conformed to the divine image. Instead, Christians are to live a re-created and renewed life in a world not yet re-created. Their lives are called to be characterized by unity and peace, established once and for all by their unity with Christ (Col 3:11-15). All are now in reality conformed to God's image and must act out the reality of that bond in daily life. Instead of lives determined by the times and seasons of the natural universe, Christians are called to live lives determined by the nature of God. This is how Christians themselves are the agents of the transformation and re-creation of the world in and through the power and the wisdom of God.

Colossians 3:18-4:1 provides a good practical illustration of this general principle. Often called *Haustafel*, or list of household duties, this section of ethical instructions offers a pattern of Christian living within recognizable structures of family and society. But the picture these verses provide of Christian family life (all the groups mentioned make up the ordinary Greek household of the time) is free of hostility, bitterness and disorder characteristic of life in a sinful world. Although we may not agree today with the social structures of the author's experience, we can concede that the *Haustafel* describes a world in miniature that is unified, ordered and peaceful. For the author, this is the world as God intended it to be. In place of a cosmic order determined by astral powers Colossians offers a social and personal moral order determined by the love of God. As they strive for justice and peace, the Christians of Colossae begin, in the Christian family and in the Christian church, the renewal of the world according to Jesus Christ, the image of God.

THE LIFE OF THE INDIVIDUAL IN CHRIST

Within the Christian family and the Christian church that are the models of unity, peace and love under God (Col 4:1), each believer is called to live out personally the reality of the fullness of God in Christ (Col 2:9). Each Christian has died to the world, yet lives the life of God within the world (Col 2:13, 20-21; 3:3). This transformation is both truly accomplished for each individual Christian in Christ (Col 3:1) and a task for each man and woman (3:5-9). Therefore, Christian life in the world is deeply "mysterious," in the most profound sense of the term.[10] The

---

[10]On the various meanings of the word "mystery" see the *Dictionary of the Bible*, ed. John L. McKenzie, S.J. (Milwaukee: The Bruce Publishing Company, 1965), pp. 595-598, or *The Interpreter's Dictionary of the Bible*, Volume 3, pp. 479-481. In its most profound usage in the New Testament, "mystery" refers to the revelation of God, either the plan of salvation in Christ or the divine nature itself.

Colossian Christians have a "glory beyond price" (Col 1:27-28; 2:3), still they must "put to death" whatever is "rooted in earth" within them (Col 3:5). They are called to growth (Col 2:6-7, 11-12, 19), rather than complacency. Their lives are to be full of joy and thanksgiving (Col 1:11-12; 3:12-15), and yet they are called to endurance (Col 1:23). They are people who know God and understand the deepest reality of the world they live in (Col 1:9, 2:2), yet they are still susceptible to error (Col 2:4, 8, 18).

They are called to be holy and pleasing to God (Col 1:10). Instead of anger, malice and deceit (Col 3:8-9), their relationships with one another must be characterized by kindness, patience, forgiveness and perfect love (Col 3:12-14). Because they are one with their Lord, Jesus Christ, who is the Lord of all creation and the giver of peace (Col 1:15-20; 3:15), their hope of fulfilling their calling is sure (Col 1:4-5; 3:4). The power they possess to do so is not theirs, but God's (Col 1:10-12).

Conclusion: Modern Spirituality in Light of Colossians

If we believe with the Apostle Paul that "Everything written before our time was written for our instruction, that we might derive hope from the lessons of patience and the words of encouragement in the Scriptures" (Rom 15:4), we know that the message of the Epistle to the Colossians is as important for us today as it was to the relatively few believers who originally received it so many centuries ago. Of course, Paul himself was referring to the words and lessons of the Old Testament scriptures in the text just cited from his Epistle to the Romans. The age-old stories, laws and prophecies of the Hebrew scriptures do remain a rich source of inspiration for Christians today just as they were for Paul. But, in the many, many centuries since the apostolic age, the writings of Paul and the other apostolic leaders about Jesus and the importance of faith in Jesus for the life of the church have become "new scriptures," the New Testament, and a source of further writings and reflection in later ages of Christianity. The letters of Paul and his disciples now provide "words of encouragement" for "our instruction" alongside the Old Testament, the only scripture known to Paul himself. It is fitting to ask ourselves, at the end of this reflection on the spirituality of Colossians, just which particular elements of our own spirituality as modern Christians are most addressed by the letter and which of the insights of so long ago are most encouraging or comforting to us now. Most of the important ideas have been mentioned in the course of our text, so this will be a review of the main points made so far.

The most important idea we encountered in the epistle was its christology—the insight that Christ was, is and always will be the absolute foundation of our reality. The world that we experience and in which we must live our lives and work out our faith and commitment as Christians is based on Christ himself. The power of God was active in Christ in creating our world and still holds it in existence through Christ alone. Our existence as Christians, the redemption of our lives from the power of evil and sin, has already taken place in the death and resurrection of Jesus Christ. The power of God is active in us, as long as we are "in Christ," re-creating us as holy, as god-like.

This christology is an idea that has tremendous power to affect our way of looking at the world and at ourselves. It can overcome the pessimism of our daily lives and the pervasive hopelessness of our culture, and replace them with hope, joy and thanksgiving, if we let it. Reflect on this for a little while. See if you really believe that these things are *true* in Christ. Now, the Epistle to the Colossians, as a part of the word of God revealed *to us* in the

New Testament scriptures, calls us as Christians to believe that all this is true *for us*. This belief must not be mere lip-service, nor can it only be something we believe about the past and in the terms of the past. To believe that would be to believe that the world of first century Colossae was safe in the hand of God, to believe that only the early Christians were re-created in God's image, holy and blameless before him. But, our world would remain jeopardized by an impersonal world and threatened by our sins. The words of the scriptures would not be *for us* and so could not affect *our* lives. On the contrary, a truly biblical spirituality calls us to believe the biblical message about *our own* world and in *our own* terms. Only then can the powerful message of the Bible really transform our lives.

Let me illustrate this with several examples. If we take the message of the Epistle to the Colossians with complete seriousness, we must believe that the world that we know—that is the twentieth-century, technological, over-populated, economically de-pressed, and nuclear-powered world—is not godless and imper-sonal, but centered in Jesus Christ in its origins and in its destiny. I seriously wonder whether or not Christians believe this. Maybe we have instead put Jesus Christ into a quiet corner of our minds and our lives, while the world outside remains completely separate from God and out of his control, and out of our control as well. Yet God is calling us clearly in the Epistle to the Colossians to believe quite the opposite—to believe that he remains in control of our world and our future through Christ—and God has been calling us to believe this for many, many centuries. For at least some of those centuries we may not have heard this message, and we might not be hearing it now.

It is not terribly comforting to believe that God has triumphed over astral demons or angelic cosmic forces such as the Christians in Colossae feared and worshipped. We don't believe in them, but we do believe in analogous dimensions of reality. We do believe in things that have the power to separate us from God, in things that have the power to hurt us, to destroy life, to end the world that we know. And we may think that God cannot, or will not, stop them from doing so. Many people today think this way. Should Christians? To feel this lack of trust and to look at the world and humankind as realities entirely removed from the power and will of God is not to take a biblical view. It is not to believe the message of Colossians. It is to be without hope in the world in spite of our Christian faith. Can we really think about the threat of nuclear disaster, for instance, in terms provided for us by the Epistle to the Colossians? I think so. The threat of the damage the astral powers might do the defenseless believers in Colossae was as real to them as the danger of what we are able to do to ourselves is to us. We, like the earliest Christians, are *challenged* by our faith in Christ, as the powerful image of God forever active in the world, to have an attitude of trust in God in the face of a perilous world. This trust must not be naive. The reality and power of evil are never denied, but they are relativized and minimized in biblical faith. There is real hope for the world because of Jesus Christ. There is a real chance for goodness in our lives because of Jesus Christ. The universe is not empty, but filled with the goodness of God because of Jesus Christ and, through our unity with Christ, because of us. To believe this is to be free of the tremendous burden we must bear if the fate of the universe depends upon us alone. To believe this is to believe in God's will to care for his own creation through his son. This biblical faith does not solve all our problems. It does not of itself accomplish all that we are called to do. What it can do, however, is change our basic outlook on reality—make it God-centered. If reality is truly God-centered, or Christ-centered as Colossians says, then we must neither worship nor fear a godless universe.

We should rejoice. We should give thanks. We should live fully within the fullness of God. We have hope.

A second important idea that we encountered in Colossians was that the world was not only created in and through Christ, but redeemed and forgiven in him. Far from ignoring the reality of sin and evil, the author of Colossians announces confidently that the power of evil has been absolutely overcome by Jesus Christ. This triumph is real at a foundational level, beyond our eyes and experience, but comes to expression in the church which is the place where the reality of Christ exists within the world. This means that unity and holiness are realities in the church. In the church as a whole—and that means in each and every Christian as all Christians come together—the power of God has forgiven our sin and transformed our life. In the church, God has created one perfect person out of all of us—Jesus Christ. Insofar as we exist in unity with one another and so in him, we are really transformed by God. We live a new and indestructible life even in the ordinary physical world. This transformation has not occurred through our own power and cannot be destroyed by our own power. Goodness and holiness are possibilities for us as individuals because of the work done *for* us by Christ and our participation in it through baptism. Our response to this can hardly be anything but profound gratitude—the "thanksgiving" that our liturgy is meant to express[11]—and an effort to make this re-creation of our lives and our world not only real but concrete.

The Epistle to the Colossians issues a strong call to all of us—those who lived in the first century after Jesus' life and death as well as those who live now—to be what we are. We are

---

[11]The meaning of the Greek word "$εὐχαριστέω$" the root of our word "Eucharist," is after all "give thanks."

re-created in God's image. We are forgiven all our sins. We are new men and women, God's chosen ones. We are members of Christ's body, totally at one with God and each other in Christ. We are therefore people who are able to live in peace. We are able to love one another, deal with one another with honesty, mercy and patience. And we do not have to rely on our own power to do it! God's power is at work in us individually and in the church, and God's power cannot fail.

Temptation is a reality in the Epistle to the Colossians. Error is a possibility. But temptation is a reality to be faced and overcome, by those who know themselves to be transformed by the power of God. Error is a possibility that can be recognized for the folly that it is by remembering the power of God as it was and is expressed in Jesus Christ and holding tight to that alone, just as the early Christians in Colossae were asked to do. We, like our ancestors in faith, must focus on the reality that is God, in which we have been given a share, and believe that evil in any form can really be overcome in Christ. As Christians we need not fear; we must hope. We must dedicate ourselves to thankfulness (Col 3:15) for what God has already surely accomplished for us in the Lord.

By living out the realities in which it believes, the church can be the focus of a transformation of society. In our families especially, as Christians, the peace and love, the mercy and forgiveness of God, should be seen in stark contrast to the disunity, strife and self-seeking that we still can experience every day on any street corner in any country in the world. The emphasis in the Epistle to the Colossians on family relationships— indeed on the family itself as a special focus—is instructive for us. The epistle seems to hold up the Christian household as the ideal expression of the way the most profound realities of Christian existence should be lived out. The emphasis on familial relationships gives great dignity to Christian marriage and families today. It is in the relationships between husbands and wives, parents and children that authentic Christian life is best illustrated. If forgiveness, peace and love characterize the Christian families in our world, our world must necessarily be transformed. Families make up the church, and the church is called upon to be God's family in the world. Therefore, in the church as a whole, the unity, love, mercy and peace that is characteristic of humanity re-created in Christ must be especially visible.

There are so many levels of meaning to be drawn out of the Epistle to the Colossians that one cannot cover them all in such a short reflection. We as Christians today are so very much like the Christians who originally received the letter. We are without our apostle. We are without the visible presence of Jesus. We have real problems, within our families, within our churches and in our world. Still, we are called to believe in the same basic message given to Paul and preached throughout the ancient world, even in the town of Colossae—a very small community in a very small world in a very small universe by our standards. We are still called to use and develop this message about God's work in Jesus Christ to solve those problems. We may often feel that we have fallen short of our stature in Christ, or that our problems are too overwhelming, or we too insignificant. The Colossian Christians probably had such feelings too. Nevertheless, the word of God, addressed to them and so to us, is a word of power, of hope, and of glory, in which our true life in Christ lies hidden waiting to be discovered anew with joy in every age.

3

The Epistle to the Ephesians

Introduction

We turn now to the Epistle to the Ephesians. It too is very probably a pseudonymous composition in the developing theological tradition of the Apostle Paul. The early Fathers of the Church witness clearly that this epistle stood in a direct line from the earlier writings of Paul and so could be called "Pauline" with no mistake. Their way of expressing this conviction that Ephesians was a legitimate descendant of the original preaching and teaching of Paul was to ascribe the epistle to him directly. Its author expressed the same conviction by using Paul's own name in the address (Eph 1:1) and again in the middle of the composition (Eph 3:1). These representatives from the early church were completely correct; there is no more "Pauline" document among the later writings of the New Testament than the Epistle to the Ephesians. They proclaimed this fact for all time in the best, indeed in the only possible, way for their time—by listing the letter among Paul's own.

But in the present century especially, as well as in the earlier critical research on Ephesians, many, many students of the epistle have noticed serious differences between Paul's authentic compositions and Ephesians. Some of these differences have to do with vocabulary and style in the original Greek of the letter. We do not need to go into specifics here. It would be helpful and interesting for you, however, in order to "get a feel for" the Epistle to the Ephesians and so give a sympathetic hearing to scholars who consider the letter pseudonymous, to read quickly through Ephesians once again. Notice the very, very long sentences, even though most translators try to break the original convoluted sentence structure into shorter segments. In Greek, Ephesians 1:3-14 and 3:1-7 are each a single sentence! Notice the frequent use of paired expressions, for example, "his will and pleasure" (1:5), "his will and counsel" (1:11), "a spirit of wisdom and insight" (1:17). Notice the frequent use of relative clauses, nouns in apposition and compound sentences, for example in Ephesians 1:9:14, 3:1-9 or 5:25-32. The net effect of the language of Ephesians, even in translation, is to give a very lofty and intellectual tone to the letter as a whole. The epistle is relaxing, conducive to profound and almost "philosophical" reflection on God's plan for us in Christ. Now read quickly through the Epistle to the Galatians, or chapters 5-10 of the First Epistle to the Corinthians. You should be struck by the differences in tone and in style. The sentences are frequently short and very direct. The tone is often urgent and highly personal. These earlier personal letters of Paul are not intended to be quiet reflections on the mystery of Christ, but solutions to pressing community problems.

This brings us to the second important reason why the majority of scholars today see Ephesians as pseudonymous. Paul was always intensely present to his communities in his letters. In fact, he used letter-writing as a vehicle for his presence and authority in churches founded by him, but left in the hands of others as he continued his missionary journeys. Furthermore, Paul was always very aware of and concerned about the conditions in his churches, about the issues and problems that troubled them and called for his help, his guidance (I Corinthians 7-8) and even his discipline (I Corinthians 5:3-4) on their behalf. Ephesians contains almost nothing of this nature. We read very little about Paul himself, except that he is a prisoner (Eph 3:1, 13; 6:20) and that he preaches the gospel (Eph 3:3-8). Surely this was generally known about him everywhere. We read almost nothing about the community which received the letter originally. We might assume on the basis of Eph 2:11-19 that the addressees were a mixed Gentile-Jewish Christian group, but beyond that we find no personal details, concrete problems, rumors or reminiscences. Now, it is certainly true that different situations call forth different responses. Paul may have preferred in his later life more general and dispassionate reflection and preaching than was possible during his earlier turbulent days as one of the pioneers in the preaching of the gospel of Jesus Christ to the Gentiles of Greece and Asia Minor. No one can say for certain that this is not so. Therefore no one can say with absolute certainty that Paul did not write Ephesians. Yet a third level of differences between Ephesians and earlier letters of Paul make it seem unlikely that he did so.

There are several key theological changes in the Epistle to the Ephesians that it seems all but impossible for Paul to have made during his own lifetime. I will briefly present only three of them because they are important, not only for the question of authorship, but for our discussion of the spirituality of the letter. First, in Eph 2:19-22 we read that the church is the holy temple in which God dwells in the spirit. Individual believers, Jews and Gentiles alike, are the building-blocks of this temple. Its foundation is the apostles and prophets (probably Christian prophets in this case), while Christ is its capstone or headstone (that is, the first stone to be laid down or the one stone that is the key to the architectural design of the building and so holds the whole structure together). The Pauline roots of this theological image of the church as a temple are clear. See for example, I Corinthians 3:16-17; 6:15-20 and II Corinthians 5:1-5, although the image is not fully developed there. For Paul himself, the temple is at once more personal (I Cor) and extra-terrestrial or eschatological (II Cor) than it seems to be in Ephesians. However, the theological development which many scholars find important is the statement in Eph 2:20 that the apostles and prophets are the *foundation* of the church. They find this bothersome because it appears to contradict a statement Paul himself makes most emphatically in I Corinthians 3:10-11.

> Thanks to the favor God showed me I laid a foundation as a wise master-builder might do, and now someone else is building upon it. Everyone, however, must be careful how he builds. No one can lay a foundation other than the one that has been laid, namely Jesus Christ.

According to this very clear text, Jesus Christ himself is the one and only person who can properly be called the foundation of the church, the temple of God. Apostles, Paul and others like Peter or Apollos, are workmen, or servants (I Cor 4:1) who help construct the temple but they are not foundational figures. It is just this danger—that of making the apostles the foundation of the church though they are only human—that Paul is arguing against in I Corinthians 1-4. It is extremely difficult to reconcile these two statements, that is, I Cor 3:10-11 and Eph 2:20, if they both come from Paul himself.

If, on the contrary, they do not both come from Paul, but Eph 2:20 comes instead from a second or third generation Christian in a Pauline church, then the two texts are not at all difficult to understand, each in its proper context. Paul's words in I Corinthians are clear. Jesus Christ is the single and unique basis upon which the very existence of the Christian church and its spiritual life rest. The author of Ephesians 2 tries to be faithful to this Pauline belief by saying that Jesus is the essential capstone or cornerstone of God's temple, the church. But, for the pseudonymous author of the Epistle to the Ephesians, the Apostle Paul has already become a figure from the past, a revered and heroic source of the faith of the author's present-day church. It is easy to see why Christians of the late first century came to see the earlier Christian apostles and prophets as the foundation of their churches, alongside Jesus Christ although never apart from him. It is an idea with which we are very familiar. Very few modern Christians would care to deny that their faith is an "apostolic" faith and their church an "apostolic" one, built on the foundation of apostles like Paul who preached and taught the gospel of Jesus Christ. Yet these same Christians would not deny that Jesus is the absolute object and basis of their faith. The later church has throughout the centuries lived with this tension that had begun by the time Ephesians was written. It began as soon as the original apostles and prophets began to die, and the church went on without a living eyewitness link to the earthly Jesus.[12]

The importance of this apparently small difference between I Cor 3:10-11 and Eph 2:20 is in reality immense. This small difference makes us see that the Christian church which received the Epistle to the Ephesians was very like all Christian churches today in one very important respect. It was a church that was called upon to reflect creatively on its own traditions, handed down from those who originally preached Jesus and the salvation

[12]A very interesting recent book by Raymond Brown, *The Churches the Apostle Left Behind* (New York: Paulist Press, 1984), explores the life the churches in the sub-apostolic era of the latter part of the first century and discusses the variety of ways in which different apostolic traditions within the New Testament itself adjusted to the loss of apostolic leadership.

which came in him. It was a church that actually did it! We will see how the author of Ephesians deepened and expanded the Pauline understanding of the mystery of Jesus Christ to create much of the ecclesiology that we know today. We too are members of Christian churches with the same calling. We too must delve into our own traditions to create new understandings of Christ, the church and ourselves which speak to our own day. We are called to remember the words of the past so that they can transform our view of the present. This book on several selected letters in the Pauline tradition is a small step in fulfillment of this tremendous task. It is comforting to know that so long ago that call was answered in such a profound way by the unknown Christian who wrote the Epistle to the Ephesians. We must hope to produce a contemporary spirituality which is equally faithful to the wellspring of scripture while honestly speaking to vital questions in the lives of contemporary Christians.

A second important theological difference between the Epistle to the Ephesians and the authentic letters of Paul, and even the earlier pseudonymous Epistle to the Colossians, lies in its description of the resurrection of Christian believers with Christ in the present life of the church. This idea is expressed in Ephesians 1:3—"Praised be the God and Father of our Lord Jesus Christ, who has bestowed on us in Christ every spiritual blessing in the heavens!", and in Ephesians 2:4-6, for example,

> But God is rich in mercy; because of his great love for us he brought us to life with Christ when we were dead in sin. By this favor you were saved. Both with and in Christ Jesus he raised us up and gave us a place in the heavens . . .

This represents an advance in the way of thinking about the resurrection and the exaltation of Jesus Christ and all Christians with him. We discussed this earlier in our study of Colossians, where we saw the beginnings of a gradual change in emphasis in the Pauline tradition. We can see a further development of this process in Ephesians.

Paul, you will remember, put a very heavy emphasis on the death of each Christian with Christ, while saying as well that each Christian also possessed new life in Christ and the sure hope of a resurrection like that of Jesus himself. The author of Colossians took this Pauline message as a given for further reflection on the mystery of Christian life. In Colossians also, Christians have died with Christ (Col 2:20). The idea is used in Colossians in a special way—to prove that those who believe in Christ are dead to the destructive influence of the cosmic forces which determine and control life on earth. Paul himself usually had a different reason for discussing the death of the Christian in union with Jesus—to prove that a believer is no longer subject to the power of sin or to the demands of the law in order to be saved. Chapters Five through Eight of the Epistle to the Romans pursue this argument in detail. The author of the Epistle to the Ephesians does not place much emphasis on participation in Christ's death, although it is very clear that it was through the death of Jesus on the cross that our own redemption came to be. We can see this, for example, in Eph 1:7

> It is in Christ and through his blood that we have been redeemed and our sins forgiven . . .

or in Eph 2:13, 16

> But now in Christ Jesus you who once were far off have been brought near through the blood of Christ . . . reconciling both of us to God in one body through his cross, which put that enmity to death.

You certainly cannot say that the author of Ephesians understands the basis of our salvation as Christians any differently than Paul, or the writer of the Epistle to the Colossians, did.

Nevertheless, when the author of Ephesians begins to talk about the life of the church and of individuals as Christians within the church, interest does not center on the death of Jesus on the cross or on our crucifixion with him, but on the glorious resurrection of Christ in the power of God and its wonderful effect on everyone who is in Christ. We have seen earlier that the Epistle to the Colossians occasionally says that those who believe in him are already raised with Christ (Col 2:12; 3:1). For that earlier letter, this resurrection is "hidden" in heaven to be revealed only when Christ comes again (Col 3:3-4). We also noticed that the Paul of the authentic letters does not express himself in quite the same way. His emphasis is on new life, but not on resurrection, in the present. The author of the Epistle to the Ephesians does not have either of these reservations. Ephesians proclaims both the present reality of the resurrection, and even the exaltation, of every Christian (Eph 2:6) and the full revelation of this previously unimaginable mystery to everyone to whom God has given the wisdom to understand it. The letter is suffused with these ideas. They are expressed, for example, in the prayer of Ephesians 1:17-20

> May the God of our Lord Jesus Christ, the Father of glory, grant you a spirit of wisdom and insight to know him clearly. May he enlighten your innermost vision that you may know the great hope to which he has called you, the wealth of his glorious heritage to be distributed among the members of the Church, and the immeasurable scope of his power in us who believe. It is like the strength he showed in raising Christ from the dead and seating him at his right hand in heaven . . .

or in Ephesians 2:4-7

> But God is rich in mercy; because of his great care for us he
> brought us to life with Christ when we were dead in sin. By this
> favor you were saved. Both with and in Christ Jesus he raised us
> up and gave us a place in the heavens, that in the ages to come he
> might display the great wealth of his favor, manifested by his
> kindness to us in Christ Jesus.

and in Eph 3:8-12, 18-21, as well as 1:3 already cited.

The mystery of the fully realized resurrected life of every
Christian in the church is one of the main theological foci of the
epistle. This tendency, already present in the Epistle to the
Colossians reaches the pinnacle of its development in Ephesians.
It is an idea we will spend quite a bit of time discussing in the
next section of our reflection on Ephesians, since it is one of
several interconnecting ideas that create the unique message of
the author for all Christians of all times. Now, however, it is
important to notice that it would be difficult to see Paul himself
as personally saying all three of these things during his own
lifetime: first, that the participation of the individual in Christ's
death through faith is of paramount importance for our salvation
from the power of sin and that resurrection is a future hope
(Epistle to the Romans); second, that we are already raised with
Christ but that our resurrected life is *hidden* in God (Epistle to
the Colossians); and third, that we are already raised up and
seated at God's right hand in heaven with Christ and that this
wondrous act of God's power and love is fully revealed in and
through the church (Epistle to the Ephesians). It is far more
likely that these three emphases belong to three different stages of
"Pauline" theologizing on the mystery of Christian life. Properly
understood, none of these positions absolutely contradicts the
others. That is what we hope to show. Each simply presents the

mystery of salvation from a different point of view, with a different audience in mind and with a different way of thinking about reality in general.

Because this is so, the Epistle to the Ephesians, standing as it does near the end of the Pauline theological tradition within the New Testament, provides an instructive model for modern Christians trying to work through a contemporary Christian spirituality with authentically biblical roots. This is just what the author of the epistle has done! The writer has thought through Paul's message about redemption in Christ and come up with some new ways of understanding its meaning at an even deeper level— ways that must have been appealing to a church living in a changed situation, ways that the church needed, ways that a particular church was ready to appreciate. This author has found a way—indeed several ways—to speak about the reality of salvation in Christ at a new level of intensity and sophistication. But most importantly, our author in Ephesians has done so in dependence upon and in utter faithfulness to the earlier Pauline tradition. As such the letter is a masterpiece of *biblical* theology and a rich resource for our contemporary biblical spirituality as Christians in a modern world.

The last of our three key theological differences between Ephesians and the earlier Pauline tradition is also one of the most creative transformations that occurs in the Epistle to the Ephesians and one of the most familiar ideas about the church for us today. Ephesians describes the church as a whole as the bride or wife of Christ (Eph 5:22-32 especially). Many of us grew up with this understanding of the church. The expression "holy mother Church" was, and still is, common. Many Roman Catholics have understood themselves as children of the church as their mother, with God as their Father and Jesus Christ as their brother and Lord. Interestingly, the idea that Christians are God's children is also very important in Ephesians, for example in Eph 5:1, "Be imitators of God as his dear children." The familial and marital structure of this ecclesiology is very significant and is the direct legacy of the Epistle to the Ephesians with roots deep within the biblical tradition. In the letters of Paul these roots lie not only in theological passages but, surprisingly, in ethical teaching as well.

The idea of the church as the wife or female counterpart of Christ occurs throughout the Epistle to the Ephesians, but it is especially clear in Ephesians 5:22-32. This is a very famous passage for many reasons:

> Wives should be submissive to their husbands as if to the Lord because the husband is head of his wife just as Christ is head of his body the church, as well as its savior. As the church submits to Christ, so wives should submit to their husbands in everything. Husbands, love your wives, as Christ loved the church. He gave himself up for her to make her holy, purifying her in the bath of water by the power of the word, to present to himself a glorious church, holy and immaculate, without stain or wrinkle or anything of that sort. Husbands should love their wives as they do their own bodies. He who loves his wife loves himself. Observe that no one ever hates his own flesh; no, he nourishes it and takes care of it as Christ cares for the church—for we are members of his body. "For this reason a man shall leave his father and mother; and shall cling to his wife, and the two shall be made into one." [Genesis 2:24] This is a great foreshadowing: I mean that it refers to Christ and the church.

We will discuss this text at length in our study of Ephesians for the variety of themes it brings together. For now it is important to see the way in which the thought of this well-known text is both a reflection on and a development of earlier Pauline texts and ideas.

The idea of the body of Christ, which occurs in Eph 5:23 and 30, is a uniquely Pauline idea which we have discussed in relation to its use in the Epistle to the Colossians. We saw that the Apostle Paul himself seems to have originated the idea, out of the common philosophical milieu of his time, to refer to a local Christian congregation in order to stress the unity of all Christians there in the single, life-giving spirit of God. We noticed that the Epistle to the Colossians combined the Pauline idea of headship with this metaphor of the body of Christ in order to defend the absolute superiority and power of Christ over his church and against all powers which might threaten or seek to dominate Christian believers. The relationship of the head to the rest of a human body seems to be the way we should imagine the relationship between Jesus Christ and the members of his church for Colossians. This is a kind of "top to bottom" way of looking at Christ and the church that certainly helped the Colossian Christians cope with the crisis they faced concerning the power of cosmic forces visible above them in the heavens.

The Epistle to the Ephesians has a different way of looking at the relationship between Christ and the church. It is described as being like the relationship between a hubsand and wife in marriage. This new understanding of the church as Christ's "wife" develops and complements the original Pauline idea of the church as Christ's body. A husband and wife are described in the scriptural passage cited by the author (Gen 2:24) as one body, one "flesh." The author of Ephesians also makes use of the insight of the Epistle to the Colossians that Christ's role toward the church is one of authority and preeminence, headship. A reflection of the *Haustafel* instructions to husbands and wives is still clear in our new text. We can, therefore, see a faithfulness to several earlier forms of tradition in the passage just cited from Ephesians 5. But we can also see that the creative process that produced Ephesians 5:22-32 has added new dimensions to the body of Christ metaphor that it did not have in I Corinthians 12 or in the

Epistle to the Colossians. We will discuss the dynamism of the new formulation of the older Pauline ideas in the following section of our study. Now we must look for the resources in Paul's own thought and letters for understanding the relationship of a husband and wife in marriage.

Paul discusses marriage and sexuality at the greatest length in I Corinthians, Chapters Five through Seven, but especially Chapter Seven. If you take the time now to read through I Corinthians 7, you will notice that his attitude toward the sexual dimension of human existence is not uniformly positive. We learn from I Corinthians 7:7 and 9:5 that Paul himself is unmarried and that he considers the unmarried state to be a superior gift from the Lord. His reasons for this preference are clearly influenced by his perception of the age in which he lives. Paul believed the second coming of the Lord to be imminent in his own day. He therefore felt the urgent necessity to preach the gospel of Jesus Christ single-mindedly and rapidly, so that as many men and women as possible might be saved from the wrath of God and the destruction it would mean for those who were without Christ on the day of that coming (I Cor 7:26-35; cf. Mark 13:7-20, 24-27 par). Paul shared this conviction of the imminence of the Lord's return with most other Christians of his time. There may have been other reasons for his preference for the single life, devoted entirely to the Lord's service, but this seems to have been a very important one. We are all aware that over a period of time Christians realized, through their own experience of the continued existence of this world without the appearance of the risen Jesus in the heavens, that the day of his coming might be indefinitely postponed according to the mysterious intentions of God. The Second Epistle of Peter, one of the very latest documents of the New Testament, is intended, among other things, to deal with questions about this experience and assimilate a new way of thinking about it (II Pet 3:1-16). If the major motivation for Paul's somewhat negative evaluation of marriage changed over a period of time and experience, might not the more positive aspects of his thoughts on Christian sexuality and marriage have come to the attention of those who followed his teachings?

The Apostle Paul does indeed have several extremely positive things to say about Christian marriage in I Corinthians 7. For example, in I Cor 7:14, he says, "The unbelieving husband is consecrated by his believing wife; the unbelieving wife is consecrated by her believing husband. If it were otherwise, your children should be unclean; but as it is, they are holy." In I Cor 7:4 he says, "a wife does not belong to herself but to her husband; equally, a husband does not belong to himself but to his wife." He goes on to say that sexual union within marriage is a good thing, to be sought rather than avoided in Christian marriages (I Cor 7:3-5). The ideas of mutuality, consecration and holiness associated with Christian marriage are very positive and have a potentially profound effect on Christian theologies of marriage. In the case of the Epistle to the Ephesians, these ideas seem to have influenced both ecclesiology and christology and their relationship to one another—as we shall soon see. But, in their context in I Corinthians Paul's positive statements often go unnoticed amid the greater number of negative, and even disparaging, things he has to say (I Cor 7:2, 9, 36-38).

In sum, it is difficult to see that the Paul who wrote the predominantly negative treatment of marriage in I Corinthians, Chapter Seven, also wrote Ephesians, Chapter Five, in which the human marriage relationship is put into parallel with the relationship between Christ and his church, and each is used to help in defining and understanding the other. At no time in his letters, except very briefly in II Corinthians 11:2—"I am jealous of you with the jealousy of God himself, since I have given you in marriage to one husband, presenting you as a chaste virgin to Christ."—does Paul himself make such a comparison. When he does do so in II Cor 11, he does not choose to elaborate on it. It is easy to understand, however, how the Pauline church of a later time might come to see the potential in Paul's positive statements on sexuality and marriage and use them to create a new theological synthesis, at once truly Paul's and truly new.

This, then, is the last of the three theological developments that make it necessary to conclude that the Epistle to the Ephesians comes, not from Paul himself, but from the dynamic and developing Pauline tradition. In discussing these three differences between the Epistle to the Ephesians and earlier Pauline letters, we have also encountered several of the most important theological ideas of the epistle. Before going on to discuss these in greater depth, only a few more introductory remarks are necessary.

Since we have seen three such significant changes in perspective in the Epistle to the Ephesians, it is not surprising that most scholars think that this epistle was written after a sufficient period of time had elapsed during which such changes could occur. Generally, the Epistle to the Ephesians is dated, by scholars who accept it as a pseudonymous composition, sometime between 80 and 95 C.E. Of course, if Ephesians had been written by Paul himself, it would have to be dated much earlier, very close to the writing of Colossians, at the end of Paul's career. We have no certain knowledge about the date when Ephesians was written, but sometime toward the end of the first century of our era seems the most reasonable hypothesis.

As I have said above, we have no certain knowledge about the writer of the epistle or about the church for which it was originally intended because of the lack of specific details about them in the letter itself. Beyond this unusual vagueness, another factor in the text of Ephesians has caused many scholars to hypothesize that it was not originally intended for a single church or a specific problem at all. Some of the very best and most reliable manuscripts of the letter omit the phrase "at Ephesus" in Ephesians 1:1. Some translations of the letter also omit the specific address, and some place it in brackets to reflect this very tradition that the epistle was not originally addressed to the Christians at Ephesus, or at least not to them exclusively. It may well have been a circular letter sent to a number of churches, or even a general epistle or treatise intended for the whole church. One group of scholars has even thought that our Epistle to the Ephesians was written by a disciple of Paul late in the first century in order to summarize the thought of his great apostolic teacher and then serve as a cover letter for the first edition of the Apostle's collected letters.[13] In any case, it is probable that Ephesians was originally intended for general consumption in the church of the late first century, and not for the church in Ephesus alone. We cannot, therefore, see in this epistle the problems and circumstances that existed in Ephesus, or in any other particular Christian group. What we *can* see is widespread trends and conditions within which the developing Christian movement existed as the earliest period of its history was coming to an end.

Just as with the Epistle to the Colossians, for the Epistle to the Ephesians the Pauline roots of the theology and spirituality of the later letter are important for its interpretation. We have already seen some of these roots in this introduction, and we will continue to encounter them throughout our study of Ephesians. One scholar in this century has said that the epistle to the Ephesians is a "mosaic" of Pauline ideas and terminology, that is, an intricate

[13]Edgar J. Goodspeed, *The Key to Ephesians* (Chicago: University of Chicago Press, 1956).

pattern created by the writer out of the individual "tiles" provided by the other known letters of Paul.[14] Within this "mosaic," however, the Epistle to the Colossians is especially important. Colossians, as we have have seen above, seems to have provided the basic outline, the key ideas and the general direction in which Pauline theology was to be developed in the Epistle to the Ephesians.

In spite of these exceptionally strong similarities between Colossians and Ephesians, there are some differences as well. Most obviously, the false teachers and the threat of false worship that were so important in Colossians do not seem to be important in Ephesians at all. We do find a warning in Ephesians 4:14 against being children "tossed here and there, carried about by every wind of doctrine that originates in human trickery and skill in proposing error." In Ephesians 5:6, the author warns "Let no one deceive you with worthless arguments." But, there are no specifics here, as there were in Colossians 2:8-23 and the argument of Ephesians does not seem to be directed as a whole against any particular error. On the contrary, this epistle is a positive development of a single idea—the church as the body of Christ—in all its implications. The threat felt in Colossians is gone, and Christians standing in the Pauline tradition are beginning to think their faith through and develop the universal vision which was always nascent in Paul's thought.

Because the writer of Ephesians reflects in an atmosphere of positive development rather than defense against attack, thoughts are free to turn in a variety of directions. We have seen that in the Epistle to the Colossians there is the threat of worship of false

[14]Ernst Käsemann "Ephesians and Acts" in *Studies in Luke-Acts*. Essays presented in honor of Paul Schubert, edited by Leander E. Keck and J. Louis Martyn (Nashville: Abingdon Press, 1966), pp. 288-297.

gods instead of, or in addition to, Christ and through him the invisible God. The epistle's response was the development of a very exalted view of Christ which placed him clearly above any other being in existence. This very "high christology" has become the premise of the thought of our author in Ephesians. It is not abandoned at any time. Yet Ephesians was not really written *about* christology. It was written *on the basis of* christology.

For several decades between the writing of Colossians and Ephesians, the church reflected on its faith in Jesus Christ the beloved Son and powerful image of God as its Lord and Savior. Gradually, Christians began to think about and write explicitly about *themselves* as participators in the reality of the Savior in whom they believed and in whom, according to Paul, they lived their only true life. They began to think about this life they lived as "church," in relation to God, to Christ, to the world and to their lives in the world. In short they began to consciously develop and articulate their own ecclesiology on the basis of Pauline christology. Not that Paul himself, or earlier Christians, had no theology of the church. Paul, as far as we know, originated the idea of the church as a body which is Christ's body. Christology and ecclesiology are ultimately inseparable. Still, during the lifetime of Paul himself and in the earlier formative decades of missionary expansion and community-building, Christian people had less opportunity to be self-reflective. They tended to concentrate much more on Jesus, his identity and his vital importance for their salvation, that is, on the basic gospel message which they preached and believed. While the development of christology went on for a very long time and Christians today are still called to deepen their understanding of the mystery of Christ, in the Epistle to the Ephesians we see the early church begin to develop a very "high ecclesiology" on the basis of the Pauline gospel and especially on the basis of the very high christology of Colossians.

Ephesians is very much an epistle to the church about the church.

The Ecclesiological Structure of Reality
According to the Epistle to the Ephesians

The preceding section ended with the thought that the Epistle to the Ephesians is a self-reflective document. By the time this epistle was written, the church of the latter part of the first century had come to know itself as it had come to know its Lord. In Ephesians this profound self-understanding comes to an elegant written expression. The church of Ephesians is conscious of itself as a reality whose very nature is described by Jesus Christ and its relationship to him. In the Pauline tradition in which Ephesians stands, one of the most important ways of describing this relationship between Christ and church was the metaphor of the body—the church was understood in the Pauline tradition as that body which is Christ's body. The identity of the church as the body of Christ is very carefully and deliberately explored throughout the letter to the Ephesians. Its identity as body of Christ has a two-fold significance: in reality and in relationship. The very nature or *being* of the church is determined by its destiny according to God's plan to be Christ's body, and the relationship between the church and all other realities—Christ, God, the world as a whole—is dictated by the fact that the church is Christ's body. To repeat: the fundamental reality and all the activity of the church are determined by the identity of the church as the body of Christ. To create for ourselves a biblical spirituality enriched by this epistle today, we need to reflect on the idea of the church as Christ's body as deeply as Ephesians does. Then we will be able to feel the tremendous impact that this idea can have on our own self-understanding as Christians. It is the spiritual heart of the letter, an idea deceptively simple yet potentially explosive. Consider whose body we are! Consider how close a bond exists between you and your own body. Is there really any difference between the two? What does this very, very close relationship between Christ and his church say about "church?" What is the best way to conceptualize this "bodily" relationship? How should the church live out its identity determined by Christ? These are the questions with which the author of Ephesians has wrestled. The answers are a legacy to the church in all times, a profound teaching on what it means to be Christian because of what it means to be Christ.

THE BODY AS A CONCRETE COSMIC REALITY

We must remember several parts of the earlier Pauline tradition in order to put the thought of Ephesians into proper perspective. Recall Paul's own use of the metaphor of the body in I Corinthians 12 once again. Paul used it to describe the necessary internal unity of the local Christian congregation in Corinth. He used it to argue against contention and rivalry. He used it with an emphasis on the spirit of God as the single life-principle of the church as church. The idea of the church as the body of Christ, its "head," was also important for the author of Colossians. Colossians used it to reassure Christians that, through their faith in Christ and their unity with him established by their membership in the Christian congregation in Colossae, they were safe from the hostile forces of the universe because of the supremacy of Christ over them. The concept of the body of Christ gave a specific expression to the hope held by each Christian for a life with God as a result of the victorious life, death and resurrection of Christ. In Colossians the concept of the body of Christ is used to describe a real unity, the unity between an earthly church and its heavenly Lord. It is an *external* kind of unity, the bond between the Lord in heaven and the fearful congregation on earth. In I Corinthians it was used primarily to describe an *internal* kind of unity among all believers in the church in Corinth. Of course, the fundamental reality of the bond between Christ and those who are joined to him in faith gave rise to the metaphor itself.

The first thing we need to realize in discussing the notion of the body of Christ as it is used in Ephesians is that it is slightly different once again. First, it is no longer a metaphor used to describe only a single local congregation either internally or ex-ternally. There is no indication in Ephesians that the author has a specific church in mind. On the contrary, several passages seem to indicate that the letter envisions a church that is world-wide, including all those who profess faith in the one Lord, Jesus Christ. Ephesians 1:10, 22-23; 2:11-19; 3:7-12; 5:23-32, 6:24 all seem to have a focus which goes beyond a particular group of Christians and speaks about *all* Christians, everywhere, as one. As our author says in closing the epistle, "Grace be with *all* who love our Lord Jesus Christ with unfailing love" (6:24). So the letter ends as it began, if the address to Ephesus is seen as secondary, "to the holy ones, believers in Christ Jesus" (1:1).

Second, and this is the more difficult point to grasp, for the author of Ephesians, the concept of the body of Christ is under-stood in a very concrete way. The author of the Epistle to the Ephesians had a decidedly philosophical way of thinking. Indeed, if there is such a thing as a philosophical treatise in the New

Testament, Ephesians may come closest.[15] Because of this somewhat abstract way of thinking about things, typical of our author,
in the Epistle to the Ephesians the body of Christ has become a
description of a concrete cosmic reality, and not only an expression
of the unity existing invisibly between Christ and those who
believe in him. The church, as Christ's body, is part of a single
whole stretching from heaven to earth. The church as the body
of Christ really exists in space—from Christ, the head, in the
highest heavens to all Christians here on earth. So, the physical
world itself is transformed and included in a concrete "body"
which is Christ himself. Try to imagine a *gigantic* human body,
reaching up to heaven, stretching across the earth, including all
men and women, encompassing, finally, the whole universe as
we know it. At the very top of this body stands Christ, the head,
above the stars; beneath him all of reality is ordered toward God

[15]The Epistle to the Hebrews also leans toward the philosophical, significantly
influenced as ait is by Platonism in its expression of the identity and mission of Jesus
Christ. Although permeated by philosophical categories, however, Hebrews is also
very much interested in the cultic system of Judaism, and in exhortation of the
Christians who received it to faithfulness to their commitment to Christ. This is
typical of the rich mixture of literary and cultural interests and backgrounds that the
books of the New Testament represent. It is interesting to notice that several New
Testament epistles caution against philosophical speculation, some form of which the
Epistles to the Ephesians and to the Hebrews themselves represent. See for example,
Colossians 2:8, ". . . see to it that no one deceives you through any empty, seductive
philosophy that follows mere human traditions, a philosophy based on cosmic power
rather than on Christ" or I Timothy 1:3b-4 ". . . warn certain people there against
teaching false doctrines and busying themselves with interminable myths and
genealogies, which promote idle speculations rather than that training in faith which
God requires." Apparently, in the first century, it was understood to be vital that a
Christian philosophy take as its absolute center Christ himself. This requirement is
well satisfied by the Epistle to the Ephesians, as we shall see.

through unity with him. This single, perfect divine/human "man" faces God in willing subjection, worship and thanksgiving. If you can imagine this (and, I admit, it takes some time to get used to this way of thinking) you will be close to perceiving the universe and the church in the way the author of Ephesians must have seen them. Consider texts like Ephesians 1:18-23:

> May he enlighten your innermost vision that you may know the great hope to which he has called you, the wealth of his glorious heritage to be distributed among the members of the church, and the immeasurable scope of his power in us who believe. It is like the strength he showed in raising Christ from the dead and seating him at his right hand in heaven, high above every principality, power, virtue, and domination, and every name that can be given in this age or in the age to come. He has put all things under Christ's feet and has made him, thus exalted, head of the *church, which is his body: the fullness of him who fills the universe in all its parts.*

and Ephesians 4:10-13, 15-16:

> He who descended [Christ] is the very one who ascended high above the heavens, that he might fill all men with his gifts. It is he who gave apostles, prophets, evangelists, pastors and teachers in roles of service for the faithful to build up the body of Christ, until we become one in faith and in the knowledge of God's Son and *form that perfect man who is Christ come to full stature* . . . let us profess the truth in love and grow to the full maturity of Christ the head. Through him the whole body grows, and with the proper functioning of the members joined firmly together by each supporting ligament, builds itself up in love.

They reveal the author's concrete cosmic perspective on the church as Christ's body. The last passage especially reminds us of the Epistle to the Colossians. Colossians had taken the first step toward this transformation from simple metaphor to cosmic reality by using it to describe the *external* unity between Christ and his church. This is, after all, a unity that stretches from earth into the highest heaven. The more profound reflection of Ephesians on this external unity can be understood as a very literal reading of the message of Colossians. In Ephesians the church has become part of the structure of reality itself as Christ's body.

As I discussed earlier, the author of the Epistle to the Ephesians is not concerned with the particular problems of a specific church. Therefore, unlike its usage in I Corinthians or in Colossians, the use of the concept of the "body of Christ" in Ephesians is not a problem-solving device. Instead, the idea that the church is Christ's body is the object of the author's reflection. Our author, and the church of the later decades of the first Christian century, asked the question that still faces all Christian churches today: What does it mean to be the body of Christ? We have examined the unusual spatial contours of Ephesians' answer to that question. Now we need to understand that answer in even more depth.

The starting-point for the answer to this question for the author of Ephesians was an understanding of Christ himself. The christology that the Epistle to the Ephesians seems to have been particularly well versed in is the very "high christology" of the Epistle to the Colossians, which we discussed earlier in this book. The idea of Jesus Christ as the image of God from all eternity, of Jesus Christ as the creative power of God in whom the world takes and keeps its very being is the christology that forms the basis of Ephesians' reflection on the meaning of the church as Christ's body. What must it mean to be the "body" of this eternal, divine and resurrected person?

THE BODY AS AN ETERNAL REALITY
THAT TRANSCENDS TIME

Let's begin by re-reading the opening passage of the epistle, often called a "eulogy" or "blessing" because of the word with which it begins. Many commentators on this epistle think that Ephesians 1:3-2:10 is an extended expansion of and reflection on the Christ-hymn of Colossians 1:15-20, which formed the hub around which our discussion of the whole of Colossians centered. If so, it is certainly a reflection taken in the direction of the church. The author consistently asks and answers the question: If this is our Lord, who are we? What does Christ mean for us, those who live in and through faith in him? In a way, the answer is simple; yet it is one of the most astounding answers ever given in the history of Christianity, to one of the most important questions. Everything that has happened to Christ has happened to us, because we are his body. Everything that he is, we are, because the church and Christ are one.

Ephesians 1:3-6 introduces us to the first stage of this glorious mystery of Christ and us.

> Praised be the God and Father of our Lord Jesus Christ, who has bestowed on us in Christ every spiritual blessing in the heavens! God chose us in him before the world began, to be holy and blameless in his sight, to be full of love; he likewise predestined us through Christ Jesus to be his adopted sons—such was his will and pleasure—that all might praise the glorious favor he has bestowed on us in his beloved.

In this text our author is recalling the marvelous works of God on our behalf *before the world began* (v. 4), and fulfilling God's intention in performing those acts of favor by giving God the praise and thanksgiving he deserves for giving such tremendous gifts to those who, of course, had no claim to them (v. 6). It is important to see the temporal focus of this first of many thanks-givings and bursts of praise which occur in the Epistle to the Ephesians. God's choice of us, those of us who call ourselves the church, occurred before the world's beginning. God's love for us began before anything at all was made. We have been blessed in heaven with every possible blessing for all eternity with God. We have always been destined to be God's adopted children—his not by natural descent, but by divine choice in love. All of these wondrous blessings are ours because we are in Christ, and *we always have been*. This is so because the Christ in whom we as church, have our being is the *eternal* Son, the image of God in the language of Colossians. Here is the faith of the church that produced the Epistle to the Ephesians, expressing to the church in all places the self-understanding of Christians who had reflected deeply on their relationship to the Lord.

Several consequences for the meaning of Christian life follow from the statements made in the section of the "blessing" cited. For one thing, the relationship between the women and men who come to God through faith in Christ and the invisible God and Father himself is not something that is new. On the contrary, it is very old, as old as Christ himself—"God chose us in him before the world began" (v. 4). It is not something that happened by accident, or was dependent on our choice, or that could have failed to happen. On the contrary, our unity with Christ, our adoption as God's children, our holiness—all of these blessings—are part of God's own, often mysterious, plan. All that we receive in Christ is done according to God's own "will and pleasure" (v. 5). This divine will has existed from all eternity. Nothing can change it or prevent its fulfillment. Our relationship with God has existed from before the world was made. We were loved by God before our birth, because Christ was loved before his birth into this world and we are part of him. Through this fatherly love that God freely gave to us, our salvation and our unity have been intended, and so accomplished, by God in Christ for all eternity.

A great deal of attention is given to the "plan of God" in the Epistle to the Ephesians (see Eph 1:5, 9-11; 3:3-6, 9-11; 5:30-32). This concern for God's will, intention or good pleasure, and power to carry out what he intends is a response or natural consequence of the belief that our salvation in Christ has existed from all eternity in the unchangeable will of God. Because our unity in and with the beloved Son of God was always God's will for us, those who have come to understand God's will through faith in Christ know that they are part of the very structure of reality itself as intended and brought about in God's own time through the creative power of God himself. Taking its being from this creative love, the church, as the body of Christ, is truly a reality that transcends time, just as it transcends space.

THE CHURCH AS A COMMUNITY REDEEMED IN TIME

Yet the church is also a reality that has come to be *in* the world and *in* time. Only recently, with the life, death and resurrection of Jesus Christ had the eternal love and plan of God for us been revealed. Only recently had the church been created precisely through the redeeming death of Christ. In Ephesians, as you can see, the nature of the church is profoundly mysterious, because it partakes of the mystery of Christ himself. Like Christ, to whom the church is joined in its very being, the church is at once a reality that transcends the categories of space and time and also a reality that exists within space and time.

The next section of the "blessing" which begins the Epistle to the Ephesians talks about the coming to be of the church in the world through the redemptive love of God expressed, as it was before the foundation of the world, in his beloved Son. Ephesians 1:7-14 speaks of the second stage in God's mysterious design.

> It is in Christ and through his blood that we have been redeemed and our sins forgiven, so immeasurably generous is God's favor to us. God has given us the wisdom to understand fully the mystery, the plan he was pleased to decree in Christ, to be carried out in the fullness of time: namely, to bring all things in the heavens and on earth into one under Christ's headship. In him we were chosen; for in the decree of God, who administers everything according to his will and counsel, we were predestined to praise his glory by being the first to hope in Christ. In him you too were chosen; when you heard the glad tidings of salvation, the word of truth, and believed in it, you were sealed with the Holy Spirit who had been promised. He is the pledge of our inheritance, the first payment against the full redemption of a people God has made his own, to praise his glory.

Here our author begins to talk about the church in a way which we find more familiar today. The church is a group of men and women, brought together by God's choice of them (vv. 11, 13), by their mutual hope in Christ (v. 12), by the forgiveness of their sins in his blood (v. 7), by their mutual possession of God's spirit given as a foretaste and a promise of salvation (vv. 13-14), dedicated to the praise of God (v. 14). But we must not forget our author's own perspective on these facets of Christian existence, i.e., that they are the revelation and expression of God's eternal will and as such are the temporal expression of a reality eternally present with God in the heavens (cf. Eph 1:3-6). It is as if in our baptism, the experience to which Eph 1:13 most probably refers, God's will for us, and so our true being, begins at last to exist in the space and time of our lives.

In using words like "redeemed" in v. 7 and in talking about the forgiveness of sins, the author of Ephesians reveals the perception that was common in the biblical tradition and very much in evidence in the Epistle to the Colossians, as well as in the earlier authentic Pauline letters: that the world and humanity are sinful and alienated from God before Christ. We discussed this theological perspective on the world at some length with regard to Colossians' reflection of it. A great deal of space is devoted in Ephesians to describing the effects of this alienation. For example, Chapter Two of Ephesians discusses the alienation and disunity that was typical of the world in the time before God's plan—to bring all things together into one in Christ—began to unfold in history.

It seems that our author has chosen the separation which existed between the Jews, as God's chosen people, and Gentiles, as those who were far from the true God, as the most important expression of this disunity. The description of Gentiles as sinners, those who follow evil spirits and worship idols, is common enough in Jewish literature of this period and we find it in Eph 2:1-2—"You were dead because of your sins and offenses, as you gave allegiance to the present age and to the prince of the air, that spirit who is even now at work among the rebellious." More surprising is the fact that the author of Ephesians, apparently writing out of a Jewish-Christian background much like Paul's own, has been like the Gentiles in sin, saying, "all of us were once of their company; we lived at the level of the flesh, following every whim and fancy, and so by nature deserved God's wrath like the rest" (Eph 2:3). It is clear that for the Christian who wrote the Epistle to the Ephesians, as for Paul before, all of humankind, whether Jew or Gentile, had been caught in a web of sin and death before the advent of God's gracious love in Jesus Christ (Eph 2:4-10, cf. Romans 1:18-2:11; 2:17-24; 3:9-20). The only possible escape from this death-trap was the divine mercy shown in Jesus, a pure gift of God's love. It was not earned or deserved by anyone, Jew or Gentile, but upon both God's overflowing kindness has come as a gift of life out of death.

If you have read the selections from Romans cited above, you can see how faithful our author is to the roots of this thought in the works of Paul himself. Paul understood the mystery of God's act in Christ at so profound a level that he could see that the gift of life out of death, or of the forgiveness of sins, was God's absolutely unique way of acting. It constituted, for Paul, a divine sort or righteousness, the only possible response to which was a gratitude to the depths of his being overflowing in praise of God's glory (Romans 11:32-36). For Paul all men and women sin, so that all may be saved from sin by God's mercy and righteousness, in order that all might give praise and glory to God in thankfulness for this righteousness as revealed to and for all humankind (cf. Romans 1:16-17; II Corinthians 4:15). True to its "philosophical" outlook, Ephesians' reflection on the universality of sin closes with a summary recalling its characteristic perception of the eternal quality of this gift arising from the unchangeable and benevolent will of God. "We are truly his handiwork, created in Christ Jesus to lead the life of good deeds which God prepared for us in advance" (Eph 2:10). For Ephesians, our "creation in Christ Jesus" is a reality before time, in time, and beyond time. It refers to our destiny in Christ from all eternity in God's will to love us in his son, as well as to our "creation" into a unity called "church" through faith in Christ. In some sense our author can say God has prepared our very deeds in advance, since all good works, as well as our ability to do them, stem from the benevolent intention of God himself.

The strong resemblance to Paul's own thought and writings allows us to presume, I think, that the author of Ephesians would have thought about the origins of sin in a way similar to the way Paul and the earlier biblical tradition thought about it. In the Epistle to the Romans, already mentioned as the Pauline background for the thought of Ephesians 2, Paul goes on to discuss the origin of sin and death in the sin of Adam and to relate the death and resurrection of Christ to the redemption of humankind from the slavery to the power of evil resulting from that sin (Romans 5:12-21; 6:12-23). Yet, our author in Ephesians does not spend any time at all discussing or describing the beginning of sin in Adam's choice of disobedience in the garden as Paul does (Romans 5:12-14; 7:7-12). We need to understand the dependence of Ephesians on Pauline ways of thinking in order to appreciate Ephesians' own understanding of sin. Otherwise we might mistakenly interpret some of the things the letter says in a way that its author would not have intended or agreed with.

For example, some very early readers tended to interpret Ephesians in a way that was not acceptable to the church as a whole.[16] This misinterpretation had to do especially with the origin of evil and the reason why sin was such a pervasive reality in human history. The Christians who came to be known as the heretical group call Gnostics seem to have interpreted the Epistle to the Ephesians to say that some men and women were created as evil, or physical, while some were created as good, or spiritual, by God or by some inferior demi-god responsible for the physical world we know but different from the God Christians worship. To read Ephesians this way is to misread it because of a lack of appreciation of its presupposition of Pauline theology. When Ephesians 2:3 says that "we . . . by nature deserved God's wrath

---

[16]For a scholarly presentation of the way such heretical groups tend to interpret Paul's letters, see Elaine Hiesey Pagels, *The Gnostic Paul* (Philadelphia: Fortress Press, 1975), pp. 115-133 on the Epistle to the Ephesians specifically.

like the rest," it presents us with a dimension of our existence which we can come to know from our experience and can understand within the biblical tradition. We know that we often fall short of even our own best intentions in many ways. We know that our lack of love and our focus on self fail to fulfill God's call to justice and mercy. We know that we were each born into a world filled with others like ourselves in these failures and live in a society which is more deserving of God's wrath than blessings. In the Bible, we are offered an explanation of these experiences of self and others which traces our collective failure to fulfill God's commandments back to the very beginning of human existence and places its origin in the will of human beings not of God.

The fact that the Epistle to the Ephesians does not spend very much time dwelling on the origin of sin and the fragmentation of humanity—even of those who were chosen from the beginning in love to be one in Christ—does not mean that the author did not have an explanation for these "facts of life," or that they were not important. Obviously the disunity and disorder of the human race before and without Christ was a major concern to this writer, since the theme is mentioned frequently throughout the letter (Ephesians 2:11-22; 3:6; 4:17-5:18; 6:10-17 especially, but also the frequent contrast between "we" and "you" throughout the letter, Eph 1:3-12; 1:13-19; 2:1-2; 2:3-5). The fact that Ephesians does not seem to find it necessary to explain the alienation and sinfulness that was characteristic of humanity and human life in the world before Christ probably means that the author possessed and accepted a traditional explanation of these dimensions of our existence, an explanation current in Pauline communities which stemmed ultimately from Paul's own writings, the Judaism of the time immediately before Christ and the books of the Old Testament.

The fact that our author thinks in another direction shows us something else as well—it shows that Ephesians is almost entirely focused on the positive dimensions of Christian life and existence. Our author knows about sin, but, rather than exploring the meaning of sin, chooses to develop the theme that sin has no place in the life of one who is united to Christ. Ephesians 5:8 illustrates this choice of focus well, "There was a time when you were darkness, but now you are light in the Lord. Well, then, live as children of light." Our author knows about the grievous historical division of humanity into Jew and Gentile—one group far from God and the other God's chosen people—but chooses to develop instead the good news that unity has been achieved in and through Jesus Christ. When Ephesians looks back into eternity, the author shows us as we were destined to be within the loving gaze of God, not as we came to be in a time and a world without Christ. Similarly, when Ephesians looks at its own time, the author shows us as we should be, or better, as we really are because of God's gift in Christ. In Christ we are a forgiven church. In Christ we are a resurrected and glorified people. In Christ we are one.

Unity as the Primary Characteristic of
the Church as Christ's Body

For the author of the Epistle to the Ephesians, it is in the church that the oneness and blessing originally intended by God to be his gift to us in his beloved Son are realized for us in our own time and in our own world. In a sinful world characterized by alienation and death, this could only be achieved by the redemptive death of Jesus on the cross, the most significant event of the second stage of God's eternal plan. Ephesians 2:11-19 reads

You men of Gentile stock... remember that, in former times, you
had no part in Christ and were excluded from the community of
Israel. You were strangers to the covenant and its promise; you
were without hope and without God in the world. But now in
Christ Jesus you who once were far off have been brought near
through the blood of Christ. It is he who is our peace, and who
made the two of us one by breaking down the barrier of hostility
that kept us apart. In his own flesh he abolished the law with its
commands and precepts, to create in himself one new man from us
who had been two and to make peace, reconciling both of us to
God in one body through his cross, which put that enmity to
death. He came and "announced the good news of peace to you
who were far off, and to those who were near," through him we
both have access in one Spirit to the Father. This means that you
are strangers and aliens no longer. No, you are fellow citizens of the
saints and members of the household of God.

It is the blood of Christ, shed in a violent and undeserved death,
that destroyed everything that functioned in our world to separate
us from one another.

The long historical separation between Jews and Gentiles
might be used here to typify all other kinds of alienation. Certainly
the division between Jew and non-Jew was very important for
the author of Ephesians, just as it was for Paul himself. The
joining of Jews and Gentiles into one church envisioned by Paul
did not happen immediately. It is very probable that Paul himself
did not live to see it happen. God's will for Jews and Gentiles to
be joined in salvation in Jesus Christ was difficult to discern in
the earliest period of Christianity. It is this hard-won insight that
Paul himself works through in Chapters Nine through Eleven of
his great Epistle to the Romans. Paul expressed his own pain that
most of his brothers, the "Israelites," had not come to faith in
Jesus as the Christ as a result of his preaching in spite of their
great blessings—covenants, promises, the worship of God in the

temple in Jerusalem (Rom 9:1-4). Paul carefully argued that God
had not abandoned the Jews to whom he made so many promises,
because God is faithful (Rom 11:1-2, 28-29). Paul believed that
the Jews had not come to faith in his own day so that Gentiles
could first believe and then Israel be reconciled to God, so that he
could save everyone—Jew and Gentile alike—by grace and
mercy (Rom 11:11-12, 22-23, 25-32). Although today we still do
not see the realization of Paul's vision of unity, we should
remember his insistence on God's absolute faithfulness to the
irrevocable promises to Israel and reflect on his conviction that
all would someday be one because of God's mercy and forgiveness.
Paul ends his argument, after all, with a hymn of praise to the
inscrutable wisdom of God. How can we grasp the way in which
this might be accomplished?

The author of the Epistle to the Ephesians was very faithful to
Paul's thought as it is expressed in Romans 9-11 in the passage
just cited from Chapter Two. In fact, we might be correct in
seeing that section of Paul's Epistle to Romans as the source for
this part of the "mosaic" that our author has created. Although
Ephesians 2 may lack the vision of Paul himself as he calls the
future salvation of Israel in Christ a giving of "life out of death"
(Rom 11:15), a true resurrection, it does describe a Christian
church in which Jews and Gentiles have become one and worship
the same God together. The images that our author uses to
describe this unity are taken from Judaism. Paul's own view of
the privileged status of Israel in the history of God's relationship
with humankind is assumed. Paul had said in Romans 9:4-5
about his "brothers" that ". . . theirs were the adoption, the
glory, the covenants, the law-giving, the worship, the promises;
theirs were the patriarchs, and from them came the Messiah (I
speak of his human origins)." The author of Ephesians draws out
the implication of those words for Gentiles during the history of

the world before Jesus— "...you were excluded from the community of Israel. You were strangers to the covenant and its promise; you were without hope and without God in the world" (Eph 2:11b-12). The presumption is that the Jews *had* hope because they belonged to a community that was close to God and to Christ, even before the birth of Jesus into our world and our history. To understand how our author would have understood this idea, we need only look back at Ephesians 1:4-5— "God chose us in him before the world began, to be holy and blameless in his sight, to be full of love; he likewise predestined us through Christ Jesus to be adopted sons..." Recall that Paul himself listed "the adoption" as one of the blessings of Israel in Rom 9:4. Looking back at the eternal dimension of the body of Christ in the light of Chapter 2 of Ephesians, we can see that our author probably was referring to Jewish Christians specifically with the use of the pronoun, "we," in the first part of the blessing that begins the letter. The eternal will of God to bestow every heavenly blessing on "us" in his own beloved Son began to be realized in our time and in our world through Israel, God's chosen people.

But this "will and pleasure" of God (Eph 1:5) is a mysterious thing, not fully revealed to Israel, not fully understood until the gospel of God's forgiveness and blessing in Jesus Christ was preached to all humankind, including Gentiles. Only in Paul's day—Paul who preached a message of salvation to Gentiles as his special mission (cf. Romans 1:5, 13; 15:15b-21; Galatians 1:15-16; 2:7)— had the plan of God been made known. Paul's disciples carried on his legacy. As our author says, "God has given us the wisdom to understand fully the mystery, the plan he was pleased to decree in Christ, to be carried out in the fullness of time: namely, to bring all things in the heavens and on the earth into one under Christ's headship" (Eph 1:9-10). The letter is even more specific about the content of that mystery, now understood because it has finally been revealed in Christ: ". . . in him we were chosen . . . ," and ". . . in him you too were chosen; when you heard the glad tidings of salvation, the word of truth, and believed in it . . ." (Eph 1:11a, 12ab). In the light of Chapter 2 we can understand our author's meaning better. God's eternal choice of us in the body of Christ included all humankind, both Jews and those who were strangers to the community of Israel. Ephesians 3:2-6 connects the revelation of the mystery to Paul's particular apostolic ministry very clearly:

> . . . to me, Paul, a prisoner for Christ Jesus on behalf of you Gentiles, God's secret plan as I have briefly described it was revealed. When you read what I have said, you will realize that I know what I am talking about in speaking of the mystery of Christ, unknown to men in former ages but now revealed by the Spirit to the holy apostles and prophets. It is no less than this: in Christ Jesus the Gentiles are now co-heirs with the Jews, members of the same body and sharers of the promise through the preaching of the gospel.

In the Pauline churches of the late first century, Paul's vision of communities in which Jews and Gentiles lived and worshiped together was becoming a reality.

The imagery of Ephesians 2 is taken primarily from the worship system of Judaism, historically centered in the temple in Jerusalem. That temple was destroyed by the Romans in 70 C.E., some years before the Epistle to the Ephesians was written, granting our hypothesis that the letter was written by a disciple of Paul late in the first century. Some early Christians certainly regarded its destruction as a sign of God's displeasure with the Jews who had failed to accept Jesus Christ as Messiah and Son of God. Our author, however, recalls the temple, and probably its destruction, in a more positive way, seeing it as a sign of the breaking down of a barrier to the common worship of God by Jews and Gentiles as one.

Historically it might be true to say that the legal and cultic systems of Judaism in a way helped to create a *division* of humanity into two hostile camps, who cherished enmity against each other in their hearts. At least that is our author's point of view. Reading the Old Testament, one cannot help noticing the negative attitude toward the ways of the nations who do not worship the God of Israel. On the other hand, reading the books of the Maccabees lets us see the cruelty visited upon the Jews by Gentile civil authority. Modern history bears witness to the continuation of this tragic hostility into our own time.

But the author of the Epistle to the Ephesians could not see into a future so marred by hatred and instead interpreted the unity in worship then taking place in Pauline churches as a reconciliation between Jews and Gentiles through the blood of Christ, whose death gave the gift of peace to both and made them into one. In the Jerusalem temple there was a wall beyond which Gentiles could not go. This wall prevented them from entering the inner sanctuary in which the worship of the true God took place. It separated Jews from Gentiles and so prevented Gentiles, as strangers to God's covenant, from having the access to God available to Jews who worshipped inside the temple. It is probably that wall in the temple which our author has in mind in writing "It is he [Christ] who is our peace, and who made the two of us one by breaking down the barrier of hostility that kept us apart" (Eph 2:14). The barrier was real, but also expressed a deeper division between the nations and God's people. In the cross of Christ, all such "walls" are broken down, so that, in our author's view ". . . through him we both have access in one Spirit to the Father" (Eph 2:18). Like the author of the Epistle to the Colossians earlier, the "Paul" of Ephesians describes this unity as the creation of "one new man from us who had been two," that is, the reconiliation of Jews and Gentiles into "one body" which is Christ's body, the church.

True to the imagery of worship and the locus of worship as God's temple in Jerusalem, the author of Ephesians can call the church a temple, a new temple built out of *people*, just as Christ's body is made up of the numerous individuals who become one in him.

> You form a building which rises on the foundation of the apostles and prophets, with Christ Jesus himself as the capstone. Through him the whole structure is fitted together and takes shape as a holy temple in the Lord; in him you are being built into this temple, to become a dwelling place for God in the Spirit (Eph 2:20-22).

This new temple of God, the church, is both like and unlike the old temple in Jerusalem. Like the old temple, it is the dwelling place of God in the midst of people. Like the old temple, the church is the place in which people have access to God. Like the old temple, it is the locus of true worship of the true God. Unlike the old temple, however, this new temple of the Lord is not a building which people may enter; it is a building which *is* people. In the church, therefore, men and women do not enter a building where God is; in the church, God enters into men and women who are a single body.[17] The spirit of God, whom we call the

---

[17]You will notice a mixing of metaphors here. The ideas of "building / temple" and "body" seem to be intermingled or interchangeable in Ephesians. This is frequently true in the writings of Paul himself, and in the intertestamental literature of Judaism as well. See for example I Corinthians 6:15-20 and II Corinthians 5:1-5 where the same mixed metaphor occurs. Notice also that the temple, the body of Christ and the spirit of God tend to be associated ideas. The explanation for this curious phenomenon is rather complex, but it has to do with God's presence in the world mediated through places of worship and, more importantly, by human beings themselves.

Holy Spirit, lives within the church. We are already familiar with this idea from the writings of Paul himself. In the original Pauline presentation of the idea of church as Christ's body, Paul emphasized the role of the spirit in relation to this unique body. The spirit was for Paul the single source of the life of the church as church and the single wellspring of all activities and gifts in the church (I Corinthians 12:4-11, 27-28). Just so, for the author of Ephesians, the spirit of God dwells in the church, providing both the unity of believers and their nearness to God. Finally, unlike the old temple, as the new dwelling place of the spirit, the church is a reality in which oneness and peace prevail over hostility, strife and separation.

The theme of unity is obviously important for the Epistle to the Ephesians in areas beyond the historical problem of the joining of Jews and Gentiles into a single worshiping community. For example, Ephesians 4:3-6 contains a brief credal statement, probably used in the Christian group that produced this epistle, which stresses unity as the leading characteristic of the church.

> Make every effort to preserve the unity which has the spirit as its origin and peace as its binding force. There is but one body and one spirit, just as there is but one hope given all of you by your call. There is one Lord, one faith, one baptism; one God and Father of all, who is over all, and works through all, and is in all.

Once again, the spirit is the ground and source of the unity that is foundational for the church. The unity of the church is a mirror of the oneness of God and the beginning and signal of the realization of his plan to bring all things into unity with himself through Christ (cf. Eph 1:22-23). The image of the church as Christ's body is never far from our author's mind. In stressing the role of apostles, prophets, pastors, teachers—in short, all roles of service and authority in this church—Ephesians gives as the goal of all the growth in faith, in knowledge and in love, the formation of the one "perfect man who is Christ" (Eph 4:11-13). It is this one person, the beloved Son of God, whose body we are as church and whom God had blessed from all eternity with his paternal love. As the church comes to know itself to be the body of Christ, loved eternally by the Father, it can come to know this love, experience it and reveal it. The church coming to know itself as it comes to know Christ, its Head, can reveal its own unity in the spirit, the authority of Christ over it and the love of the eternal Father in the world. It is to this task that the church is called in Ephesians.

Unity in Love: The Task of the Church as Christ's Body in the World

The third and final stage in the mysterious plan of God to be fulfilled in the body of Christ is only hinted at in the "blessing" which begins the Epistle to the Ephesians. It cannot be fully described since it is the full realization in our created universe of time and space of the peace, order, unity and love which has existed in God for all eternity in the heavens. Ephesians 1:10, ". . .the plan he was pleased to decree in Christ, to be carried out in the fullness of time: namely, to bring all things in the heavens and on earth into one under Christ's headship," and Ephesians 1:23, ". . .the church, which is his body: the fullness of him who fills the universe in all its parts," allude to this full realization. It has certainly begun, with the death and resurrection of Jesus Christ and our participation in them (Eph 1:20-21; 2:4-7). The realization of God's plan can all be seen and is known by those with the wisdom that comes with faith in Christ (Eph 1:17-18). It is begun in the church, Christ's body. But in our world the fullness of time has not yet come. Therefore the church as the body of Christ in the world exists as the sign of the working of divine power, the agent of the outpouring of divine love in the world. The church, as Christ's body, must itself accomplish the revelation of God's good will and pleasure to all and so transform the world—not, of course, through its own strength, but in and through the enabling power of God (Eph 2:10; 6:10-17). The re-creation of the world that is the task of Christ's body is not a magical transformation, although the church is called to act in and through the creative power of its head, Jesus Christ. This transformation of the fundamental structure of reality into conformance with divine love is to be accomplished through the "life of good deeds" lived by those "brought to life with Christ" (Eph 2:4-10). It is an ethical transformation which reveals the plan of God. A full three chapters of the Epistle to the Ephesians are devoted to ethical, or moral, instruction. These chapters are a call to the church to live out its collective life in a way that corresponds to the reality of its existence as church and so fill the world with the presence and power of God. The church is called to manifest the gifts of the life given to it in Christ and to reach out toward the world from the wealth within itself. Chapter Four of the letter begins with this call: "I plead with you, then, as a prisoner for the Lord, to live a life worthy of the calling you received, with perfect humility, meekness, and patience, bearing with one another lovingly" (Eph 4:1-2).

The goal of the life of the church in the world is, first and above all for the author of Ephesians, the preservation of the unity of the body of Christ which is created by the presence of the Spirit within it. On the basis of this divinely established unity, the life of the church should be marked by peace as its most important quality (Eph 4:3). Such peace is the natural result of lives lived out together with love for the other as the constant guiding principle directing all activities, all offices and all ministries within the church as the body of Christ (Eph 4:11-12, 15-16). As members of the church learn to live lives characterized by unity, peace and love, they "grow up" as children of God. They begin to live the lives intended for them for all eternity by God, their Father in Christ (Eph 5:1; cf. Eph 1:3-6; 2:10). They begin to transform the world according to the will of God.

The life of the church as a whole, as a body, must be a life in which truth, kindness, compassion and forgiveness are the rule. In the church there is no place for lying, anger, bitterness, slander or malice of any kind. There is nothing lewd, or obscene— nothing whatever unclean—in the body that is the church (Eph 5:3-18 passim). Of course what is true of the church as a whole must also be true of the lives of the individual members of the body. The focus of the Epistle to the Ephesians is not on the individual believer, however; it is on the church as it is a unity. For Ephesians the church is, in a way, a whole that is greater than the sum of its parts. This is so because, as the body of Christ, the church is a reality created through the will of God, established by the action of God in Jesus Christ and living by the power of God in the Holy Spirit. As such, the church is not simply defined as the total of its membership, although its membership does make up the church. There is divine dimension to the church in Ephesians, yet this is not at all the same as saying that the church itself is divine. The church is united with Christ as his body in the most profound way imaginable and so is holy. Yet this is not the same as saying that the church is identical with Christ.

The author of the Epistle to the Ephesians tries to express this very mysterious, very elusive, idea in a variety of ways. We have already discussed several of them. The church is a reality that has existed eternally in the will of God, yet the church has come into existence in time. The church is a reality that transcends spatial categories, since it partakes of heavenly blessings while living out its life on earth. The church is the body of Jesus Christ and so shares in the resurrection and exaltation of its Lord, yet it is made up of individuals who are born, must suffer and will surely die as all of humanity has always done. The church is a single body living in peace, unity and love, made up of individuals who may fail to live up to this ideal. The church is holy (Eph 5:3), yet must be exhorted to strive for holiness.

The holiness of the church is an extremely important idea in Ephesians. The holiness of the church is grounded in its relationship to Christ, is the direct result of Jesus' sacrificial death on behalf of the church, and is made present in the church to the degree that the church lives in imitation of that sacrificial love of Christ. In the lives of individual Christians, if they truly embody the unity and peace that must be characteristic of those who are "children of God" (Eph 5:1), the will of God from all eternity is realized at last in time and space. God's wisdom, love and holiness are revealed in and to the world through the church. As Ephesians 3:10-11 says, "Now, therefore, through the church, God's manifold wisdom is made known to the principalities and powers of heaven, in accord with his age-old purpose, carried out in Christ Jesus our Lord." Notice the reminiscence of Colossians here in this reference to the principalities and cosmic powers. Although they do not play as important a part in the thought of this letter as they did in Colossians, these personalized forces of the universe are still called upon to witness the triumph of God's love within humanity through Christ and his church, his body. The third and final stage of God's plan for us in Christ is still being completed as the church grows into the "fullness of God" by accepting the consecrating love of God in the person of Christ and living a transformed life in accordance with the pattern provided by the death of Jesus for the sake of the church.

THE BODY AS RELATIONSHIP:
THE MARITAL IMAGERY OF EPHESIANS

The ideas which we have discussed as the most important elements of Ephesians' contribution to the self-understanding of Christians are the church as the body of Christ; unity, love, peace and holiness as the primary characteristics of the church; and, finally, the church as part of the fundamental structure of reality itself according to the plan of God. These elements are intertwined in a unique way in Ephesians 5:22-33. We have already cited this passage in the introductory section of this chapter as one of the best known and most influential parts of our epistle. We have also discussed the traditional roots of Ephesians' theological synthesis in the letters of Paul himself. Now, at the end of this presentation of the "ecclesiological" spirituality of the letter, it is important to look at Ephesians 5 once more. In this short passage the author of Ephesians has given us perhaps the greatest theological gift contained in the letter. The "Paul" of Ephesians begins to talk about the concept of the body of Christ, provided to him by the earlier Paul, in terms of realtionship.

If you take the time to re-read Ephesians 5:22-33 now, you will see that it is a very beautiful text, but one that is also extremely dense, that is packed tightly with different images and theological ideas. Perhaps having read these pages on Colossians and Ephesians you are now able to sort some of these ideas into different categories according to their earlier separate uses. For example, you already know that the church was described as Christ's body in I Corinthians 12 and the Epistle to the Colossians. This idea has been the focus of our study of Ephesians so far. What is unique about this passage, however, is the variety of other images and ideas that are associated with the body metaphor. Some of them are familiar. For example, the idea that Christ is the "head" of the church, his body, was typical of the use of the concept in Colossians. You can recognize, too, the instructions to wives and husbands as part of the Colossians' *Haustafel* (see the subsequent instructions to children and fathers in Eph 6:1-4 and to slaves and masters in Ephesians 6:5-9). So, this profound teaching on the relationship of the church to Christ as body is inserted into the middle of fairly commonplace ethical instructions. From our introduction of the passage earlier in this chapter you also know that Paul's own ethical teaching regarding Christian marriage, in its more positive aspects, was probably used to amplify Colossians' more stereotyped and culturally determined understanding of the relationship. It is clear that Ephesians 5:22-33 is a multifaceted text, a very good example of the "mosaic" created by the "Paul" of Ephesians. It even contains a quotation from the Old Testament. Verse 31 cites Genesis 2:24, part of the story of the first man and woman and their union as husband and wife. This first "marriage" described in scripture is, according to our author, profoundly mysterious. It refers, at the deepest level of its meaning, to Christ and the church (Eph 5:32).

When a New Testament writer cites a verse from the scriptures, or even a part of one, it is always a good idea to look at the context of the verse cited, that is, the surrounding few verses both before and after it, to get the full message or story that the author had in mind. This is especially necessary for the citation in Ephesians 5:31 which begins with the words, "for this reason...." For what reason? Why do men and women become one when they marry? If you look now at Genesis, Chapter Two, verses 18-25, you will see the context that is helpful in understanding the thought of Ephesians Five. You will notice that Genesis provides several ways of understanding the reason why a man and a wife become one body in marriage. For example, they separate themselves from others, even their parents, as they join to one another exclusively (Genesis 2:24a). Also, it is not good in God's eyes for a person to be alone (Genesis 2:18). It is better, according to this archetypal story about human origins and human nature, for a man and woman to be joined in partnership. (This is an interesting contrast to Paul's own statement in I Corinthians 7:1b, "A man is better off having no relations with a woman," made under the influence of the impending second coming of the Lord.) But the most important reason in the eyes of the very ancient Genesis tradition for the unity of a man and woman that marriage brings about is given in verses 21-23 of Chapter Two, the most proximate context of the verse our later author has cited in Ephesians. It is because of the primeval and original unity of man and woman which marriage re-creates and replicates.

> So the Lord God cast a deep sleep on the man, and while he was asleep, he took out one of his ribs and closed up its place with flesh. The Lord God then built up into a woman the rib that he had taken from the man. When he brought her to the man, the man said: 'This one, at last, is bone of my bones and flesh of my flesh; this one shall be called "woman," for out of "her man" this one has been taken.' That is why a man leaves his father and mother and clings to his wife, and the two of them become one body. (Gen 2:21-24)

This is the full text that our author in Ephesians would like us to consider when we try to understand the citation in Ephesians 5:31-32. Sometimes this story from Genesis is interpreted to refer only to a presupposed subservience of women to men. After all, Eve is taken from Adam's body and so is derivative from him. Adam names his wife and so is in authority over her. These ideas may indeed have been in the mind of the compiler of the Book of Genesis and in the minds of the people who cherished and retold this story for centuries before it came to be in the form we now have it. These people lived in a culture in which women frequently did live as less than the equals of their husbands. The author of Ephesians also lived in such a social world and probably would have agreed with that point of view. We can see this in the teaching about submission and authority in Eph 5:22-24 and 33 which make a frame for the author's more important ecclesiological message. But we can ask today whether or not it is necessary to interpret Genesis in this way. Possibly the idea of inequality comes just as much or more from the reader's presupposition that to be given one's being from another is to be inferior to that other. Is that really the case? Isn't the emphasis of the Genesis story, on the contrary, the equality and similarity of the man and the woman because of their original unity? Doesn't Genesis mean to tell us that Adam and Eve were suitable partners because they were the same bone, the same flesh, the same body although separate?

It is this interpretation of the story that is most important to the understanding of Ephesians Five. It is because a man and wife are one flesh, *one body*, that they can be compared to Christ and the church as one body, and not because one, the husband, is in authority over the other, the wife, even though the concept of authority is certainly one dimension of the passage. Think about our study of the body of Christ as the idea is expressed in Ephesians. The primordial unity between Christ and the church in which we were blessed in the heavens before the world began (Eph 1:3-5) is like the orginal unity of the man and woman in creation. Like Adam and Eve before God took Adam's rib to form the woman and filled its place, Christ and the church were originally one. Now, men and women are separate, but they can join together again to become one flesh in marriage. Just so, in time the church came to be in the world. It came to be made up of the many men and women on earth, just as Jesus Christ was born and died to rise again for our salvation. The men and women who live in the church are not identical with Jesus Christ, yet they are the body of Christ. The church is a unity in and with Christ created in and through love. The author of Ephesians needed to find a way to express this different kind of unity of body, of oneness, that is in the world rather than before the world's foundation.

Again Genesis offers the key to understanding this mystery. Men and women, like Adam and Eve, create and express a new kind of bodily unity in marriage. This being "one flesh," or one body, in marriage is not a unity of identity, but a *relationship*. This relationship restores and express the reality of the original unity of man and woman in being, a unity that is not broken in creation but only transformed. The author draws a clear parallel between the unity of a man and a woman in marriage, that is, between a husband and a wife, and the unity of Christ and the church as one body. Like the unity of marriage, this unity of Christ and the church is a relationship, a unity both gracious and voluntary constituted in and through love. Like the "marriage" of Adam and Eve in the garden, the relational unity between Christ and the church is based upon and is the reflection in time of the primordial unity of all of us in Christ according to the will of God.

Ephesians does not leave this relationship we call the body of Christ unspecified, nor does the author allow it to be finally described by the culturally determined matrimonial customs of the first century, or, for that matter, of our own century. On the contrary, Ephesians 5 uses the self-sacrificing and consecrating death of Jesus Christ as the pattern for defining the relationship of love between Christ and the church, as well as between husbands and wives within the church. In a way our author turns the tables on the earlier procedure, as we have been describing it, of looking back to the older tradition of the scriptures to find the mystery of Christ and the church already fore-shadowed there (Eph 5:32). Now the recent events of Christ's death on the cross begin to dictate the proper understanding of that foreshadowing. Having come this far in our study of the Pauline tradition, we can see that the tradition of the past is constantly in dialogue with the faith and experience of the present, so we should not be surprised to see the same process once again. In the central section of this important passage which is about the nature of the church and about the behavior of wives and husbands in Christian families at one and the same time, the author of Ephesians defines both as relationships of self-gift in which all parties participate.

One could say that for Ephesians the body of Christ, as well as Christian marriage, are relationships completely characterized by love. That would be correct. But love is such an over-used word in our modern vocabulary, we have to be careful to define it as our author does. Ephesians 5:25 defines love—"Husbands love your wives, as Christ loved the church. He gave himself up for her . . .;" so does Ephesians 5:29—"Observe that no one ever hates his own flesh; no, he nourishes it and takes care of it as Christ cares for the church." The reason for and result of such love is given immediately, " . . . for we are members of his body" (Ephesians 5:30). The love of Christ for the church, the members of his own body, is a consecrating kind of love. This love makes the church holy, purifies it, redeems it, glorifies it (Eph 5:26-27). Husbands are to mirror this self-sacrifice, this kind of care and nourishment, in their relationships with their wives. Surely the submission of wives to their husbands "in everything" calls for nothing less. The effect of this mutual imitation of Christ's gift of himself, even to death for the other if this be necessary as it was for a humanity lost in sin, will be a holiness of life and a mutual consecration such as Paul himself envisioned in I Corinthians 7:14-16. In the case of Christ and his body, the church, this mutual love is nothing less than God's redemption of the world in Christ and the revelation of the body of Christ in time and space, a mysterious unity of transforming love that has reshaped the world for those who believe.

Conclusion: Modern Spirituality in Light of Ephesians

We have now explored the Epistle to the Ephesians using its most important idea—the church as the body of Christ—as a way to unlock the thought of this great epistle and get in touch with it from a single consistent perspective. There is no doubt that Ephesians is a very profound reflection on the church—on its nature and on its relationship to Christ. As we have said, the reality of church for the author of Ephesians is a reality that is dependent on the reality of Christ. Our nature as church is determined by his nature as Son. Our lives as Christians are dictated by his life as savior. There is no doubt either that Ephesians' transformation of christology into ecclesiology is often difficult to understand and at times unfamiliar to us when we probe the text to find out how its author might have understood the ideas which each passage preserves and speaks constantly anew to Christians. Nevertheless, as was the case with the Epistle to the Colossians, the Epistle to the Ephesians is a rich resource for the spiritual life of Christians today. It issues a challenge to the church of the present and of the future to strive toward theological reflection that is able to match the depth and beauty of its own. Ephesians calls us too to keep before our eyes the vision of the church as Christ's body, for it was this relationship that was the self-identity of the very early Christian community that created it. Finally, Ephesians urges all who can see in the church of today the pure and glorious partner with whom Christ himself is "one flesh" in love to live up to this vision in their daily lives as Christians in the church and in the world.

Our study of the Epistle to the Ephesians has revealed its author's dependence on many earlier theological ideas, that can be found both in the Old Testament and in the earlier letters of Paul. By getting to know this single epistle better, we have become acquainted with other parts of the biblical tradition also because of this constant tendency to repeat and reuse the tradition of the past. This is as it should be, since as modern members of the ancient Judaeo-Christian religious family we must constantly renew the memory of our common heritage. We have also seen, however, the creativity of the author of Ephesians in handling that tradition. Ephesians shows us one very dynamic way that Christians have worked with their heritage in the past. Besides reverently repeating it, just as we do in prayer, worship and teaching, Ephesians has developed a new and deeper understanding of the mystery of the plan of God for our salvation. This new understanding came in part from combining ideas, which were originally separate parts of the author's heritage, into a new unity. The result of this synthesizing of traditional ideas in Ephesians has been some of the most enduring and important development of the Pauline tradition in the New Testament period. The magnificent combination of sexual or marital imagery with the body of Christ metaphor, which we have just finished discussing, is a fine example of this process at work.

We have seen too, in the course of our study, that the

author's philosophical way of looking at the world made a difference to the Colossians in which a common cosmology, or way of understanding the structure of the universe, had a great deal to do with the way its author understood and described Jesus Christ. In Ephesians also, the common philosophy of the day as well as the social customs, in the *Haustafel* of the ethical section of the letter for example, have been important in the author's way of understanding and expressing the reality and life of the church. For example, the author of Ephesians was comfortable with seeing the church as the kind of a body that transcended the mundane categories of space and time and reached instead into the heavens and into eternity. This was possible in the age of Ephesians in part because of the Platonic and Stoic philosophical systems which we have mentioned only briefly here. These ways of thinking were familiar at that time and provided our author's fundamental way of looking at the world and so also the framework into which faith was articulated. It may not be possible for us to understand the reality of the church *in the same terms* as our author did. In fact, the very names "Platonism" and "Stoicism" are strange to many people today. We do not know these systems of thought and so they do not shape our world. We *cannot* use the same path then, as did the author of the Epistle to the Ephesians, to articulate for ourselves the relationship between our faith, derived from the epistle itself among other sources, and the world in which we live. Yet this kind of articulation is the task to which all Christians at all times are called. It is a task which we have watched the author of Ephesians perform in a faithful yet creative way. The answers of Ephesians to the questions we ourselves must answer about our self-identity as church, about our relationship to Jesus Christ, about the plan of God both *are*, and *are not* our answers. Our study of the Epistle to the Ephesians poses a dilemma for us, and offers an invitation.

The many profound theological ideas presented by the Epistle to the Ephesians, which we will have to summarize so briefly here in this conclusion, *are* our ideas. As part of our scripture, the Epistle to the Ephesians is the word of God for us, the revelation of God's message about Jesus Christ, about us and ultimately about himself. Yet we are not necessarily at home in the universe, or the thought-world, or the society into and through which this revealed message was articulated. We have our own society, with its own questions, customs and demands. We have our own ideas about the universe and how it works, about the origins of human life, about so many things that form a coherent whole for us and constitute the universe of meaning in which we live and think and act. We have worked very hard to reconstruct and understand to even a small degree that universe of meaning which was the stage upon which Christians of the first century walked and talked and from which they can and do speak to us the words of God. I hope the effort has been fruitful, and now you can see and hear more clearly the message of Ephesians about the reality and meaning of the church. But here is the dilemma. For the author of Ephesians the church is truly a reality that transcends time, transcends space, lives in a dynamic relationship of love with Christ so that its very existence is described by unity with him. Because this is what the epistle teaches, we believe it. We are called to believe it, challenged to believe it, consoled by believing it. And we are also called to think about it, ponder it and make it truly a part of our world and truly effective in our lives. But, where are the ideas about time and space which will help us in our time understand and make our own this deeply mysterious nature of the church? The Epistle to the Ephesians alone cannot and will not answer this need. We must answer our questions ourselves, in a faithfulness to our tradition as profound and creative as was that of the author of Ephesians.

It is beyond the scope of this small volume to begin the answering. It has been our purpose here to speak the biblical word, loud and clear, so that we may know the tradition to which we are called by the example of Ephesians to complete and creative faithfulness.

This great "mosaic" of Pauline tradition invites us to create our own theological "mosaic." We are challenged to engage in the loving transformation of our biblical heritage, not from Ephesians alone but from the full scriptural witness of both Testaments, into a truly biblical, yet contemporary faith and theology. We can only be encouraged in our own endeavor by the success of the "Paul" of Ephesians in doing just that. In Ephesians God has not given us only a revelation of the reality of our existence in Christ's body, of his plan from all eternity to love us in Christ, and of all the other theological riches contained in this great epistle. This would have been a great enough gift, but we have also been given a pattern to follow in receiving and speaking that same theological message today. Even more than that, God has given us reason to be optimistic about the task to which we are called for the sake of our biblical faith. Look at how beautifully the word of God has been communicated in Ephesians! Consider what potential for deepening our understanding of ourselves lies at our fingertips within the New Testament. Think about how profoundly the person of Christ and the unity which is church could be expressed in terms of first-century culture, language and thought! To begin our own theological journey we need only ask which of the many important truths revealed in Ephesians are most important, which have we made the least use of or forgotten, which are most needed by our world? And we are on our way.

Clearly the most important insights that Ephesians has to offer to Christian people today are ecclesiological. Ephesians is indeed a letter to the church about the church. What are the most important things that we can learn, as church, from this epistle?

First of all, we can learn that the church is one. For the author of Ephesians the church is a reality characterized both externally and internally by unity—externally, because the church exists only by being the body of Christ, that is, by being one with Christ in the closest possible way—internally, because the church as the body of Christ must live in imitation of his own complete sacrifice of self. Only such a mutual gift of selves can hope to truly unite us. We have not thought very much about the individuals who are members of the church in this chapter on Ephesians. That is because the author did not think "individualistically" as we frequently do today. To be sure, in the first century, as in our own day, many individual real people made up the church. Yet our author did not choose to focus on us as individuals with our unique needs, rights and duties. Instead Ephesians speaks out of a vision of the church as a whole, and sees us as individuals only as we personally partipate in the blessings and obligations that come to us because we are one. Moreover, the church in Ephesians is not a divided church, but a universal church. This is in sad contrast to the divided Christianity that we know today. The author of Ephesians would have found the separation that now characterizes the experience of Christian churches impossible to imagine. How can the living body of the beloved Son of God be divided up? This is a question we are challenged by the Epistle to the Ephesians to ask ourselves today. The church of Ephesians is a universal church, a single body in which previously hostile groups were reconciled at last and brought together to worship. For our author, this unity is the revelation of the will of God. How can Christians today fail or refuse to worship together since Ephesians witnesses to that will? How can hostility or anger ever be characteristic of our relationships *within* the church? This great epistle issues a powerful call for unity and peace among and within Christian congregations and radically calls into question our reasons for separation, whether individual or ecclesial.

Second, we can learn that the church is holy. Because of its unity with Christ, the church as a whole and in each of its members is redeemed, resurrected and actually alive with new life (Eph 2:4-7). The church has been purified by the sacrifice of Jesus Christ in his death on the cross (Eph 5:25-27). Therefore, the church is truly sinless, truly glorious, truly spotless, because forgiven through the power of God to forgive. The church is enabled to live in imitation of this sacrifice of Christ and the merciful love of the Father which it expressed. Indeed, it is the mission of the church to do so (Eph 5:1-2). All children are able to act as their parents act, and indeed are expected to do so. All of us were destined for adoption, and in the church become in fact truly God's children in the world. So, the god-like behavior of the church in the world is the revelation to the world of God's love, God's truth, God's peace, God's mercy, and also of God's power—just as what our children do speaks more loudly than any words about what we are like as parents and as people. The church is able to live this life of holiness and we are able to do the deeds of mercy, love and peace to which we are called because all of this is *God's* "handiwork." Our very lives are "created in Christ Jesus" to be lived in the power of God.

It is obvious from this description of the life of the church, and of all who are within it, that for the Epistle to the Ephesians the reality of "church" is more than what we can see or experience the church to be. The letter talks about the church in a very idealized way. We can mean any number of things when we say the word "church." We can mean a building in which we worship. We can mean a particular group of people who identify themselves as a unique believing and worshipping community, as, for example, the United Church of Christ or the Roman Catholic Church.

We can mean the governing body of our church, or its teaching authority, as Roman Catholics do when they say, "the church teaches." But for Ephesians the church is still much more than all of those things combined. Through its unity with Christ, which the author has tried to express using the Pauline idea of church as Christ's body, the church is joined to the reality of God. This dimension of the church's existence can never be absolutely limited to the church as it is experienced in our day-to-day lives, yet it can never be absolutely separated from the church of our experience either. So, the church really is all the things that the Epistle to the Ephesians says it is—holy, united, peaceful, the revelation of God's way of loving us in the world. *We* ourselves are really all those things! Yet, the church really is as we experience it. We, as the church, know that we are not perfect. We sometimes sin. We often fail to behave with the love, mercy and peace that yet truly characterize the church.

This is the most difficult part of the message of Ephesians for us to understand and to believe. We have tried to express it here in a variety of ways. We have said that for Ephesians the church is a reality that transcends our categories of time and space. We have said that the church is truly Christ's body, existing in a union with Christ that is unimaginably close, that touches the very heart of its reality. But, to put the idea in its simplest possible form, we could say that the message of Ephesians is that in Christ we are more than we seem to be. When we are one, we are one with Christ. When we are one, we are transformed by God's love and enabled to live as children of God.

We are challenged by the Epistle to the Ephesians to believe that this is so. We are challenged to accept our destiny and our identity in Christ. The message of Ephesians is one of hope, for those who are sometimes discouraged by their own failures and inadequacies, or by the inadequacies and failures of others who are also Christians and so also "church." We are all familiar with the all-too-human faces of the church. We can sometimes be scandalized because of things done in the course of history of which we can scarcely be proud today. We can despair because someone in a position of leadership makes a mistake, tells a lie, or leaves the church. We can be "turned off" because Christians sometimes don't behave with justice or mercy or peace or love. Still, the author of Ephesians calls out to us with the voice of God ringing in the words that the church is holy and we are holy in the church. Truly this epistle was written for our consolation (remember Romans 15:4).

The Epistle to the Ephesians places the church at the very center of reality. It tells us that our lives in Christ were part of God's creative plan from eternity. Often today we think that religion is not an integral part of the world, but something entirely different, coming from and having to do with another dimension. Frequently enough, it *is* just that as we live out our lives, something on the fringe of our daily existence. Maybe we belong to the church on Sundays, but the rest of the time we belong to the world. For the author of Ephesians this could never be the case. In our study of the Epistle to the Colossians, we learned that Christ is at the very center of reality, and we were invited to let that kind of faith transform our world before our very eyes. In this study of Ephesians we have learned that the church is also at the very heart of existence, with a key part to play in the destiny of the world. We are invited to allow that kind of self-identity to transform ourselves and, through us, our world. In the church the love of God enters our dimension and is revealed to the world. Knowing this, we are called to live as we truly are, carrying on the revelation of God's love in our families (Eph 5:22-6:4) and in our communities (Eph 4:25-32).

Lastly, it is fitting to end this reflection on the Epistle to the

Ephesians with the idea that should be the most important part of the response of the church, indeed of every individual believer, to this message of love and hope: thanksgiving. The epistle begins with a blessing, an extended prayer of praise to God for the many gifts of love given freely to us in Christ (Eph 1:3 ff.). This praise is repeated throughout the letter and is described as the goal of God's plan in Christ (Eph 1:6, 14, 16; 3:20-21). God has blessed us, made us one, raised us up to new, spiritual life with Christ so that we might praise his wondrous mercy and goodness. The idea of thanksgiving and praise as the proper attitude of those who believe in the gospel of Jesus Christ was also important for the Apostle Paul himself (see II Cor 4:15 for example). Sometimes we become so focused on the benefits that we receive from God that it does not occur to us that gratitude rather than relief, or pride, should be our immediate response. It might strike us as strange that the goal of God's activity is not *us*, but *himself*. Yet, for the author of Ephesians God is obviously and most importantly the one to whom praise and thanksgiving should constantly flow from those who have been given a share in Christ's life and God's love without deserving it (Eph 2:8-10). This is so obvious, yet we have such a tendency to forget it. We have a tendency to ask for more, although we have already been given everything in Christ. In a way, the Epistle to the Ephesians is the embodiment of the author's praise to God by recounting all those wondrous gifts already given. Yet, we are the real beneficiaries of the author's blessing. Because we have learned through this written witness more about God's unimaginable plan to bless us in Christ, we are enabled to pray to God as we should—we, who now know who we are in Christ, thank and praise you, Father.

Part Two
The Pastoral Epistles

4

I Timothy, II Timothy and Titus

Introduction

The second part of our study of several letters in the tradition of the Apostle Paul will focus on a group of three brief letters addressed to individuals, the First and Second Epistles to Timothy and the Epistle to Titus. Only four letters within the Pauline letter corpus are addressed to individuals. The Epistle to Philemon is the fourth. It may be worthwhile to discuss Philemon briefly here as a way to highlight the distinctive character of the Pastoral Epistles through comparison with a similar literary work. If you take time right now to read all four of these short letters, you will very quickly realize why the letters to Timothy and Titus form a separate and distinct trio among the Pauline epistles[18] and why the letter to

---

[18]We are cautioned, however, by scholars now working on the Pastorals not to assume that they are identical with one another, or that they all have the same author, if Pauline authorship is doubted. See Luke Johnson, *The Writings of the New Testament*, p. 382, for example. This is indeed good advice which encourages us to value each letter in itself and appreciate its individual emphasis and contribution. We will try to keep this caution in mind in this chapter. Nevertheless, the Pastoral Epistles are also clearly similar in many respects and do represent a unique type among the Pauline letters. Therefore we will treat them together here and use the term "author" rather loosely to refer to the person, or persons, who composed them and the churches they represent.

Philemon is not grouped with them, even though it is a letter certanly written by Paul himself and, at least primarily, directed to an individual Christian believer. Since you have already read the Epistle to the Colossians and the Epistle to the Ephesians and studied them carefully in the earlier chapters of this volume, some other important contrasts with those letters will probably occur to you immediately.

PHILEMON AND THE PASTORALS

The names of Timothy and Titus are familiar to readers of the New Testament. Timothy is mentioned by Paul himself in several of his letters (II Corinthians 1:1, 18; Philippians 1:1; 2:19-23; I Thessalonians 1:1; 3:1-8; Philemon 1:1) as one of his co-workers. Titus is also mentioned as several times acting as Paul's messenger to his established communities (II Corinthians 2:12-13; 7 and 8). The story of the early church told in the Acts of the Apostles bears out the impression of Timothy as a close companion and assistant to Paul on his missionary journeys (Acts 16-19). However, Philemon was not a missionary companion of Paul and is not otherwise well known to us. These individuals—Philemon on the one hand, Timothy and Titus on the other—present a definite contrast that is typical of the letters in which their names appear as addressees. As co-workers with Paul, Timothy and Titus were involved with the foundation and organization of churches. As his messengers during Paul's lifetime, Timothy and Titus probably acted on Paul's authority and according to his instructions. The letters to Timothy and Titus have to do with just these two things above all: the handing down of Paul's authority within his churches and the structure and character of those churches. In contrast, Philemon was an individual believer converted by Paul (Philemon 19) to faith in Christ, who receives in his letter advice and admonition from the Apostle about a critical decision he must make in his own life. It is amazing that such a personal message has survived and been preserved for us. It allows us to see Paul in a private moment, and certainly his advice to one Christian has immense value for all Christians. But, the Epistle to Philemon is not directed specifically to the governance of the church as those to Timothy and Titus are. The Epistles to Timothy and Titus have long been grouped together under the name, "the Pastorals," precisely because their message concerns the character and duties proper to pastors, that is, those who are responsible for the care of the church.[19]

In the closely related themes of apostolic authority and church life, the Epistle to Philemon on the one hand and the Pastoral Epistles on the other do not seem to be very similar. This second level of contrast is especially striking in the area of authority. In the letter to Philemon, Paul is extremely subtle in using his authority as an apostle and the one who brought Philemon to faith, and therefore life, in Christ. He prefers, he says, to *appeal* to Philemon to accept a runaway slave back into his home as a brother in Christ out of the love all Christians should bear one another in the Lord (Philemon 8-10). Paul is also responsible for the conversion of the slave, Onesimus, to Christian faith. There is no doubt that Paul's authority over

---

[19]For a very understandable and reliable short commentary on the Pastorals among other later New Testament letters, see Jerome H. Neyrey, S.J. *First Timothy, Titus, James, First Peter, Second Peter, Jude.* Collegeville Bible Commentary 9 (Collegeville, Minnesota: The Liturgical Press, 1983), on the present point especially pp. 7-9. See also Robert J. Karris, *The Pastoral Epistles,* New Testament Message 17 (Wilmington, DE: Michael Glazier, 1979).

both Philemon and Onesimus is real. He knows that he can command; he prefers to appeal. His appeal is powerful but indirect, rooted in the respect in which Philemon holds him as the apostolic founder of his church.

The Pastoral Epistles make a much more direct appeal to the apostolic authority of Paul. The source of that authority lies, as it did in the Epistle to Philemon, in Paul's status as the one who first preached the gospel of Jesus Christ in the communities which he now has placed in the care of Timothy and Titus and those chosen by them in turn. The Pastoral Epistles, however, are interested in overt appeal to that authority to ensure the correct preservation of the faith of the churches in terms of creed, the proper behavior of members of the churches in terms of accepted social and moral norms, and the regular transference of that authority in terms of rituals such as the laying on of hands (I Timothy 4:14). These letters do not display the subtlety of the Epistle to Philemon in referring to Paul's authority. Indeed, it is the conscious purpose of the Pastoral Epistles to make certain that the teaching they contain is reinforced with the apostolic authority of Paul and thus more likely to be approved and obeyed.

The content of that teaching in the Pastorals is difficult to compare with that of the Epistle to Philemon, since Philemon is concerned with only a single issue: slavery and the decision Philemon must make as a Christian in a particular response to it. On that single question, though, the contrast is interesting. In Philemon, Paul handles this issue with a great deal of finesse and with a subtlety parallel to that with which he brings his own authority to bear on the conscience of Philemon in this letter. Paul sent a runaway slave, whom he had encountered in prison and had given the invaluable gift of faith, back to his owner carrying the epistle as a sort of "cover letter" giving instructions about how he was to be received. So, it might seem that Paul, and the letter he sent, are supportive of slavery as a social phenomenon and institution. After all, Paul sent the slave Onesimus back into a life of slavery to Philemon. He didn't tell Onesimus to run away again, or keep him by his side in prison. Did he approve of slavery then? Should Christians today approve it? Paul apparently didn't try to change it.

A look at I Corinthians 7:20-24, 29-31 confirms that this attitude toward slavery was typical of Paul and that his action in sending the slave back to his master is not unexpected. I Corinthians, Chapter Seven, also gives the reasons for Paul's opinion. He believed, as we have mentioned before, that the world was shortly coming to an end in the return of Jesus from heaven as judge. He believed that conditions in this present world made little difference, since they were so briefly to be endured, and that the life of the Christian in Christ was all that counted in this world or the next. In all likelihood, the slave Onesimus would have been returned to his owner forcibly anyway. Since Paul very probably made his acquaintance in prison, Onesimus was returned by law as a captured runaway with or without Paul's volition. In sending his letter, therefore, Paul was not so much participating in the return of the slave, a matter about which he had little or nothing to say, as he was doing all that he could do to ensure that Onesimus would be received by his master in the world as a brother in the Lord.

In his letter Paul urges Philemon to behave toward his slave with the love which he has and shows for "all God's people" (Philemon 4-5) and which comforts Paul in his imprisonment (Philemon 7). Paul implies that the escape was providential because, following his capture, Onesimus was converted to

Christianity through his contact with Paul in prison (Philemon 15-16). Paul asks that Philemon treat this slave as a brother, not a slave, because both have been given a new life and a new stature as Christians through Paul's preaching of the gospel to each of them. Paul appeals to Philemon to accept Onesimus back into his home as he would receive Paul were he to arrive there for a visit (Philemon 17-19). You can imagine what sort of treatment that would be! Paul would be warmly welcomed as an honored guest. He is asking a great deal of Philemon in this letter. He is asking nothing less than a complete transformation of his normal way of looking at the realities of life in the world. In the world, Onesimus did not deserve respect, love, or a warm reception. In fact, a very severe punishment might have been exacted by the owner of a runaway slave. In Christ, however, Paul is willing to have Onesimus' guilt charged to his own account, in order to have the slave welcomed as he would be himself. So, while on the surface it seems that the Epistle to Philemon is supportive of slavery, in fact Paul is calling for a reversal of the attitudes and behavior toward slaves that make slavery possible in a society. This transformation of a slave into a brother can only lead, eventually and inevitably, to the end of slavery among those who are united as brothers and sisters by a common faith in Christ.

The Pastoral Epistles also discuss the behavior of slaves who are Christians. After reading the profoundly liberating message of Paul himself, we are liable to be disappointed in the viewpoint they express. I Timothy 6:1-2 and Titus 2:9-10 are the texts to look at for a comparison with Philemon. For example, the first letter to Timothy says

> All under the yoke of slavery must regard their masters as worthy of full respect; otherwise the name of God and the church's teaching suffer abuse. Those slaves whose masters are

brothers in the faith must not take liberties with them on that account. They must perform their tasks even more faithfully, since those who will profit from their work are believers and beloved brothers.

A sharp admonition to teach nothing at variance with this "teaching proper to true religion" follows immediately (I Tim 6:3).

You can easily see that the point of view in this short text just cited is not quite the same as those expressed by Paul in Philemon and I Corinthians, Chapter Seven. The author of I Timothy is speaking to the slave rather than to the master, as Paul was in Philemon. This alone would make the message sound different, of course, but there is a greater difference than can be accounted for that way. This text does not speak about the equality of the slave and the master in Christ, nor does it speak about the love that each should bear the other as a brother in Christ (or a sister in the case of female slave and mistress) as an active force in their relationship or as its determining factor. Love between Christian brothers and sisters may be supposed from the phrase, "beloved brothers," in verse 2, but the author refers to it only to reinforce the demand for respect and labor already inherent in the worldly relationship of slaves and masters with the "good work" of Christian fellowship superimposed upon it. The slave should be glad to work hard because a fellow Christian, rather than a pagan, will benefit. Indirectly the Christian community will benefit. We miss the transforming power of Paul's appeal for love in Philemon—a love that ultimately shatters the barrier between master and slave.

Moreover, the motivation for the slave to remain a slave is very different in I Timothy than it is in I Corinthians 7:20-24, even though Paul himself would have given the same advice.

For Paul worldly status did not matter. Nothing worldly mattered in a world that was passing away. For I Timothy, however, the world matters. This positive attitude toward the social world in which the church lives out its life in Christ is typical of the Pastoral Epistles. Indeed, it is one of their distinguishing characteristics. I Timothy 6:1, in providing the motivation for slaves to behave in exactly the way the society of the time expected a slave to behave, gives expression to a fundamental stance toward society as a whole. If a Christian slave does not behave with respect and work diligently, then the reputation of the Christian church and the message about God and Christ that it preaches will be damaged. Society will conclude that Christians are lazy, or dangerous to the status quo, out to destroy the system of values believed and practiced by those outside the church. I Timothy 6:1 implies in its teaching about slaves that the Christian church must function within society, must value and live amicably within the world in which it finds itself. This is a very important shift away from Paul's disregard of the world and all existing social structures. We have already mentioned that by the end of the first century, most Christians had come to realize that the second coming of the Lord might be indefinitely postponed. In the Pastoral Epistles this realization resulted in a change of perspective on the value and usefulness of the church's inter-action with the world of its experience.

It is because of differences like these between the Pastoral Epistles and the genuine Epistle of Paul to Philemon, in the use of apostolic authority or the attitude toward slavery as an expression of the proper Christian relationship to the structures of this world, that most scholars do not consider the Pastoral Epistles to be the work of Paul himself. Many other aspects of these letters also reveal that they are probably the work of a

Christian of the very late first century or the very early second century of our era. We should not be surprised that these letters sometimes sound very different from Paul's own writings. Christianity itself had changed a great deal by the end of the first century of its existence. We must expect a corresponding difference in the writings produced by the second- or third-generation churches of this later period, when they are compared to the letters of the newly commissioned Apostle to the Gentiles. It was not the world that had changed, nor society. We have seen that Paul and the author of the Pastoral Epistles both had to deal with the social institution of slavery, for example. Both had to deal with marriage (I Corinthians 7:1-16, 25-28, 32-40; cf. I Timothy 2:8-15; 4:1-5; 5:3-16), with political power (I Corinthians 5:9-6:11; Romans 13:1-7; cf. I Timothy 2:1-4; Titus 3:1-2) and with social custom (I Corinthians 11:1-16; cf. I Timothy 2:9-12)

We must be careful to notice too that Paul's own position on some of these issues resembles that of the later Pastorals. No clear line can be drawn between Paul himself and the Pastorals on every issue. For example, Romans 13:1-7 recommends to Christians an extremely cautious and positive attitude toward political authorities and structures. Here he is very similar to the "Paul" of the Pastorals. Paul's own responses to the problems, issues and needs facing his early churches are so marvelously varied that it is impossible to force him into a single mold—either the freedom-loving, non-conformist social critic or the well-behaved, avuncular solid citizen. We must take seriously Paul's own statement in I Corinthians 9:19-23:

> Although I am not bound to anyone, I made myself the slave of all so as to win over as many as possible. I became like a Jew to the Jews in order to win the Jews. To those bound by the law I became like one who is bound (although in fact I am not bound

> by it), that I might win those bound by the law. To those not
> subject to the law I became like one not subject to it (not that I
> am free from the law of God, for I am subject to the law of
> Christ), that I might win those not subject to the law. To the
> weak I became a weak person with a view to winning the weak. I
> have made myself all things to all men in order to save at least
> some of them. In fact, I do all that I do for the sake of the gospel
> in the hope of having a share in its blessings.

As he says, he has an overwhelming concern for the gospel and
for enabling as many as possible to live through its saving
power. There is room for all men and women, *as they are*,
within this salvation. Paul will adapt himself to them for the
sake of the gospel. Paul himself will change, and change again,
although he will never change the truth of the gospel (Gal
2:5). There is room in the Pauline church for many viewpoints
and many emphases, because the most important thing is not
one's viewpoint, but the truth of the gospel and the life of the
church. There is room in the Pauline tradition for both the
theological reflections of the Epistles to the Colossians and the
Ephesians and the pastoral exhortation and instructions of the
Epistles to Timothy and Titus. They too are the legitimate
heirs of the Paul who was "all things to all men," the Paul who
cared for the believer's salvation in Christ and life in the
church above everything else, the Paul who could respond to
change. And, there was change.

A CHANGED CHURCH IN A NEW AGE

It was not the world that changed. It was the church. With
a growing new self-identity came new perspectives, new needs
and a new awareness of the relationship between the Christian
and the world. Christianity began with a tremendous explosion

of missionary activity, especially among the Jews who lived outside of Palestine and then among Gentiles of Greece and Asia Minor. Paul himself was part of that missionary impulse. All of his letters come from a very early period in the life of the church, from approximately 48-60 C.E. At that time Christianity was a small movement, not yet separate from the ancient religious traditon of Judaism which gave it birth. It was made up of a series of small groups, sometimes widely separated from each other geographically, which met in the homes of their leading or founding members. Such small groups were at first invisible, and for a long time unimportant, to Graeco-Roman society and the far-reaching political power of the Roman Empire. Christianity seemed to be, and for a time was, indistinguishable from Judaism to outsiders.

In the last third of the first century of our era, however, Christianity became an increasingly large movement. Christian churches became larger and more numerous. A clear and final separation between those who believed in Jesus Christ as the Son of God and those within Judaism who did not share this faith occurred, and Christianity and Judaism became two distinct religious movements. The continued existence of the world and the delay of the return of the Lord in glorious and terrible judgment were accepted as part of the plan of God. These various changes began to have profound effects on the lives of Christians and on their ways of thinking.

For example, the delay of Jesus' return in glory meant that the church began to recognize that it would exist in the world for a long time, not a short time as Paul and many first-generation Christians had thought. This meant that society could not be ignored, but was something that Christians would need to live with, and within, for the indefinite future. Any large group of people needs organization and structure if it is going to endure and be productive for anything but the very briefest time. So, we see in the Pastoral Epistles a very strong concern for structures, procedures, and offices that was not present in the letters of the missionary Paul.[20] Once the Christian churches were differentiated from Judaism, they found themselves without the system of worship and its ready-made patterns that Judaism had evolved over its long history. The church began to develop its own identity as a worshiping community. Large groups, in contrast to small ones, tend to attract the attention of political authorities when they meet regularly. The Roman Empire was suspicious of groups which did not fit into established and customary religious or social systems and was nervous about its continued political dominance. Therefore, we see in the Pastorals a very strong concern for "appearances," for the way the church, as well as the behavior of individuals within the church, might be viewed by outsiders, especially those with political power. Christian groups could no longer depend on the tolerance which had traditionally been extended to Jews.

All of these changes taken together have produced, in the Pastoral Epistles, a message about Christian self-identity and about the life of the church within its social world that is distinctive, different in many ways from the message of Paul himself and even from the other pseudo-Pauline epistles such as Colossians and Ephesians, and yet authentically Pauline. We have already seen some of its tendencies in the comparison of the Pastorals with Paul's letter to Philemon. We saw a concern with the way the behavior of Christian slaves would be understood by outsiders. The advice given in I Timothy to

---

[20]This is a case in which the letters differ. II Timothy does not emphasize structure, although I Timothy and Titus do.

slaves, for example, was intended to create a positive, rather than a negative, view of the church in the minds of those who were not Christian. We recognized that this implied a positive view of the world on the part of the Christian author who wrote the letter. In the course of this chapter, we will encounter other changes in perspective. There is a new focus on the individual within the church, rather than on the church as a whole. There is a deepened appreciation for the destiny of those who do not believe in Jesus Christ, who are outsiders to the church, in the plan of God. The idea of the universal salvation of humanity as a whole assumes more importance.

As we walk into the world of the Pastoral Epistles, we will meet Christians who are quite different from those men and women who were addressed in the letters we have studied earlier in this volume. We may, however, be meeting Christians who are rather more like ourselves than any we have encountered so far. As Christians of the twentieth century, we may find ourselves more at home in the church of the Pastorals than we would have been in Colossae, for example, if we could suddenly be transported there. In many ways, but not all ways of course, the church of the Pastorals is our church as earlier Pauline churches are not. In part this is because the Pastoral Epistles deal with issues of daily human life and experience more than with theological ideas. So, they answer questions very like our own. Then too, we are still living in a church like the church which produced the Pastorals in significant ways. For example, we are still separated from Judaism. We still hope for the second coming of the Lord, although we wonder if it might be delayed for an indefinitely long time. We pray, as Christians at the beginning of the second century might have done, that our neighbors who do not share our faith might come to the blessings of life in Christ.

We struggle to integrate our faith in him with our day-to-day lives in politics, in business, and in society. We strive to get along with each other. We are confused about the roles that women and men should play in church life. We look to our leaders for example and guidance, just as they did so very long ago. In many ways, as we read the Pastorals we are reading about a familiar church. We are coming home.

The Relationship Between the Pastoral Epistles and the Epistles to the Colossians and Ephesians

THE PROBLEM OF FALSE TEACHING

The Pastoral Epistles do not break new theological ground. We will not encounter any new and unfamiliar theological ideas here, as we did in the Epistle to the Ephesians for example. In fact, the author of the Pastorals sees a danger in unrestrained theological speculation. For example, I Timothy 1:3-4 instructs Timothy, as the agent of the Apostle Paul, to stay in Ephesus "in order to warn certain people there against teaching false doctrines and busying themselves with interminable myths and genealogies, which promote idle speculations rather than that training in faith which God requires." Similar warnings are repeated in I Timothy 1:6-7; 4:7; 6:3-5; II Timothy 2:14-18, 23; 4:3-4; Titus 1:9-14; 3:9-11. False teachers seem to be a problem in the communities of the Pastoral Epistles. The threat of false teachers was also a very important factor in the articulation of the relationship between Christ and the cosmos that we saw as the heart of the spirituality of the Epistle to the Colossians. In Colossae, however, there was a difference in the false teachers as well as in the response of the author to the challenge they posed for the faith of the Christian community there.

We might begin our study of the Pastoral Epistles by contrasting them with Colossians and Ephesians, studied in Part One, to demonstrate the development and character of the tradition of the Apostle Paul. This will, I think, lead to a more focused appreciation of the major interests of the Pastorals themselves. The Pastoral Epistles disapprove of unrestrained theological development. The Epistle to the Ephesians offers one of the most sophisticated and highly developed theologies in the New Testament. There is a clear contrast between the Epistle to the Ephesians and the Epistles to Timothy and Titus on the question of theological thinking within the Christian churches. It is interesting to notice that in the text cited from I Timothy, he is instructed to remain in *Ephesus* to warn against idle speculation and false doctrines! Perhaps the city of Ephesus was known to house Pauline churches with a keen interest in theological speculation upon the original message of Paul. Perhaps enough time had passed so that the Epistle to the Ephesians had become associated with the city as it now is, even if it was not originally sent there exclusively, and the author of the Pastorals was reacting to later developments of its "philosophical" ecclesiology. Since we do not have much certain information about the dating, destination or authorship of any of the epistles discussed here, we can never know for sure the exact course of events that led to their composition or their precise interrelationship. Nevertheless, thinking about these letters in the Pauline tradition from this point of view allows us to see both the variety that existed within even a single apostolic tradition during the New Testament period, and the acceptance of differing viewpoints that our unified canonical New Testament represents. The coexistence of diverse points of view on important questions within the church of the New Testament, as illustrated within the canonical collection itself, is an important element in a spirituality today which grounds itself in the New Testament.

Of course, it is by no means correct to see the Epistle to the Ephesians itself as the kind of false teaching which the Pastoral Epistles are intended to curtail and oppose. The church's acceptance of the theology of Ephesians through its inclusion, alongside the Pastorals, in the New Testament would certainly preclude this. Many scholars say that heretical gnostic systems, rejected by the church, and known to us now from the later Nag Hammadi literature recently discovered, are the object of the polemic of the Pastorals.[21] We know that the Epistle to the Ephesians was very popular with these later heretical groups which interpreted it in ways that the church of the second and third centuries could not accept.[22] Therefore, the Pastoral Epistles are reacting to an *abuse* of theological speculation, or to an *excess* of it, while the Epistle to the Ephesians provides us with a model for an acceptable way of theological thinking about Paul's message in a later age. The relationship between these two strands of Paul's tradition is, therefore, quite complex. The fact that both strands are preserved for us today offers modern Christians a profound teaching about the life of

---

[21]See Reginald H. Fuller, "The Pastorals," in *Ephesians, Colossians, 2 Thessalonians, The Pastoral Epistles*, pp. 105-107; C.K. Barrett, *The Pastoral Epistles*, (Oxford: At the Clarendon Press, 1963), pp. 12-18. For English translations of the heretical texts in question, see *The Nag Hammadi Library*, ed. James M. Robinson (San Francisco: Harper & Row, Publishers, 1977).

[22]Pagels, *The Gnostic Paul*, p. 115.

the church. A dynamic tension exists between two different impulses inherent in Christian existence. The church's life is lived within and between creative alternatives established by the New Testament itself. In the Epistle to the Ephesians we have seen a beautiful example of theological reflection on the church as the body of Christ from eternity through time and into the future. In the Epistles to Timothy and Titus we are warned that unrestrained theological speculation is dangerous if it separates us from the fundamental message taught from the beginning by the apostles. For it is this that the author of the Pastorals offers as an alternative to the "false doctrine" which results from excessive speculation: the careful and faithful handing on of the message about Christ which brought the church into existence in the first place (I Timothy 1:11, 15; 2:5-7; 6:20-21; II Timothy 1:13-14; 2:1-2, 11-14; 3:14-15; Titus 1:9). Today we have a great deal to learn from both of these viewpoints. We are doubly fortunate to have had them both preserved for us. From Ephesians we learn that it is important, and beneficial, for the church to reflect on the gospel message of the mystery of Christ in order to create a constantly renewed understanding of it in every age. The Pastoral Epistles remind us, however, that the proclamation of our redemption in Christ given in the apostolic age remains a constant reference point for our own efforts to express for ourselves the meaning of God's act in Jesus Christ. His life, death and resurrection and the original proclamation of these events and their significance are the fundamental data of all theology in New Testament, as well as contemporary Christian, churches.

In the matter of false teachers, too, the difference between the Pastoral Epistles and the Epistle to the Colossians leads us to consider a fundamental attitude of the Pastorals and to appreciate it better because of the contrast. In the Epistle to the Colossians, false teachers had come from outside of the church bringing a message about ritual worship of cosmic forces that was not reconcilable with, but inimical to, worship of God in Christ. The author of the epistle responds to this as an attack on the apostolic message about Jesus Christ as the Lord of the universe. The church is always liable to influences from outside its faith and its community, which are not compatible with its self-understanding or with its faith. Frequently throughout history in responding to the challenge of unbelief or misunderstanding, Christian thinkers have dug deep into their tradition and their experience of God in Christ and the Spirit to produce a new, more clear and more profound expression of the faith that was challenged. So, the experience of the author of Colossians is often replicated in the lives of other, later Christians. Each of us has probably had the experience of reaching a better understanding of our own faith by trying to explain it to someone else.

If you review the passages listed as references to false teachers in the Pastorals, however, you will see that those who are preoccupied with speculation or teach false doctrine are not outsiders, from different communities or from outside of faith in Jesus Christ entirely as unbelievers. The false teachers in the Pastoral Epistles seem to be insiders, members of the very same communities which the letters are meant to reach. The response of the "Paul" of the Pastorals is therefore different from the response of the "Paul" of Colossians because the situation is so different. The author of the Pastorals does not need to deepen or expand the theology of these communities. The problem is much more concrete. It is a matter of how these Christians who make up the churches of the late first-century of our era are to *behave* as Christians. Even more specifically, the "Paul" of the Pastorals must decide about the way Christians are to *think* as Christians. Most particularly, our author tells us what sort of Christian is to *lead* the church into the second century of its existence. This question of Christian leadership is vital here because, as we have seen, the church of the era of the Pastorals was growing up and so in need of the self-identity and coherent structure that sound leadership can provide. The issue of leadership is also urgent because the churches addressed through and represented by Timothy and Titus, companions of the Apostle Paul himself, are being called on to decide between two differing types *within their own membership*—those who adhere strictly to the apostolic message as it was traditionally formulated and passed down in their churches and those who departed from that message in search of theological development beyond its scope. We must presume that the author of the Pastorals could not see the theological message of the false teachers as rooted within the Pauline gospel, which was foundational for the church. Beyond this, however, the "Paul" of the Pastorals saw the false message as yielding poor results in terms of ethics, or the behavior of those who espoused it.

It has been an important task of this volume to seek out the wellspring of Pauline theology within these few epistles we have studied by tracing their ideas back into the authentic writings of Paul himself. In doing this we have been following a path that the author of the Pastoral Epistles would have approved, and in fact points us toward, when he speaks as Paul, in such passages as II Timothy 1:13-14.

> Take as a model of sound teaching what you have heard me say, in faith and love in Christ Jesus. Guard the rich deposit of faith with the help of the Holy Spirit who dwells within us.

In the course of our study of Ephesians and Colossians we have seen the heritage of Paul creatively preserved in the face of challenges and within new categories of thought. We have seen too that even when theological reflection on the message of Christ seems to be of paramount importance, the expression of faith and the outgrowth of theology in behavior that is in harmony with Christian moral standards has never been neglected. Faith and theology yield acts of love, especially for the more "theological" Epistle to the Ephesians. The literature of the New Testament is quite consistent in insisting that a tree is known by its fruits, and that the inner life of Christian faith reveals itself in action. In the Pastorals this becomes the major focus. The Pastoral Epistles do not discuss Christian action in an abstract way. They illustrate it through the use of specific examples and carefully describe the type of people who make up the church and the kind of behavior that should be characteristic of them. In the Pastoral Epistles we have a practical guide for Christian life and leadership in the world in which we live.

A RICH AND COMPLEX TRADITION

Several striking similarities between the two epistles we have studied in Part One of this volume and the Pastorals—apparently so different in content and in aim—will illustrate the complexity of their relationship in more theological matters and the riches afforded by this complexity for modern Christian spirituality. You remember that it was extremely important in the Epistle to the Colossians to reject an ascetic lifestyle—one that required abstinence from certain foods, for example, or required observance of certain ritual actions or seasonal festivals—as essentially idolatrous and so inappropriate to Christian faith. I Timothy 4:1-5 contains a very similar message—

> The Spirit distinctly says that in later times some will turn away from the faith and will heed deceitful spirits and things taught by demons through plausible liars—men with seared consciences who forbid marriage and require abstinence from foods which God created to be received with thanksgiving by believers who know the truth. Everything God created is good; nothing is to be rejected when it is received with thanksgiving, for it is made holy by God's word and by prayer.

As in Colossians, such false asceticism is associated with demonic spiritual powers under whose sway the "false teachers" of this message have come. The "image of God" christology of Colossians is not mentioned here, but the solution to the problem is the assertion that God's creative power has determined the character of the world we live in and through it all things are good. We should probably think of the many times in the first and second chapters of Genesis when, following a creative act, God sees his creation and finds it good. For example, Gen 1:20-22a,

> Then God said, "Let the water teem with an abundance of living creatures, and on the earth let birds fly beneath the dome of the sky." And so it happened: God created the great sea monsters and all kinds of swimming creatures with which the water teems, and all kinds of winged birds. God saw how good it was and God blessed them...

and Gen 1:24-25,

> Then God said, "Let the earth bring forth all kinds of living creatures: cattle, creeping things, and wild animals of all kinds."

> And so it happened: God made all kinds of wild animals, all
> kinds of cattle, and all kinds of creeping things of the earth. God
> saw how good it was.

probably express the reason why the author of I Timothy
rejected abstinence from any particular food. All the animals
which we use for food are good in God's eyes and according to
God's word in scripture. We can see very clearly that the tone
as well as the reasoning of this passage are quite different from
Colossians, Chapter One and Two, and yet the message
remains essentially the same.

Paul himself rejected abstinence from certain foods as an
essential part of the Christian gospel (see Romans 14:1-23; I
Corinthians 10:14-33). He did so out of an overwhelming
concern for the unity of the church which far outweighed any
distinctions which could be made on the basis of what could
or could not be eaten. In reading these passages from Romans
and especially I Corinthians, we can see the precedent for the
way that I Timothy solves the problem, since Paul himself
quotes the Old Testament to justify his answer to the same
question, "the earth and its fullness are the Lord's" (I Corinthians 10:26, citing Ps 24:1 cf. Pss 50:12, 89:11). We can also see,
in I Corinthians 10:14-22, that for Paul ascetic practices in
matters of food and drink were associated with worship and
with questions about the relationship of the emerging Christian
communities to other, older systems of worship and the idols
and demons he saw as the objects of pagan worship. So in the
attitudes and writings of the Apostle Paul himself we can also
trace ideas similar to those that come to full expression in the
Epistle to the Colossians.

In the matter of abstinence from marriage, the relationship
between the Pastoral Epistles and the thought and writings of

Paul himself can be seen to be as complex as that between the pseudo-Pauline Colossians and I Timothy. The author of I Timothy clearly approves and recommends marriage as the ideal Christian life-style, and disapproves of those who forbid it and recommend an abstinence from marriage and thus sexual relations for Christians, not only in the passage cited, but also in other places in the letter (I Timothy 2:15; 3:4-5, 12; 5:14). It is certainly true to say that the Apostle Paul did not "forbid marriage" and so would not have been among those condemned by the author of I Timothy as a man "with seared conscience." Nevertheless, we have seen that the Apostle Paul recommended a single life devoted to the preaching of the gospel and service to the Lord as the ideal Christian way of life in view of the imminence of the Lord's return (I Corinthians 7:1, 7-9, 25-35, 38, 40). Paul does not seem to think of marriage as a state in life that builds up the community in the way that the author of I Timothy obviously does. In fact, it is on precisely this point that our two "Pauls" differ. For the Paul of I Corinthians, those who are married are concerned, quite naturally and unavoidably, with things of "this world." This is not beneficial to them or to the church because "the world as we know it is passing away" (I Corinthians 7:31). The "Paul" of I Timothy looks at "the world" in a significantly different way and so evaluates marriage somewhat differently. For this "Paul" marriage is good in the same way that all foods are good and for the same reason. We can tell that this is so because the ideas of abstinence from marriage and abstinence from foods are paired in I Timothy 4:3 and discussed together. Marriage was created by God and so marriage is good.

A glance at the Book of Genesis, out of which we explained this author's attitude toward food, confirms that this is so. In Genesis 2:18 we read, "The Lord God said: 'It is not good for

the man to be alone. I will make a suitable partner for him.'"
Here in the older biblical tradition there is a basis for including
marriage among those things that God's creative activity has
given to humankind to be received with thanksgiving. The
Apostle Paul himself knew this tradition, and it probably
accounts for the fact that he did not forbid marriage and did
have some extremely positive views on it that we have seen
developed in the Epistle to the Ephesians, Chapter Five. For
Paul himself, however, this created good of the "world as we
know it" was to be set aside in view of the end of the old world
soon to be accomplished in the Lord's return from heaven.
While the author of I Timothy also expects the Lord's return
(I Timothy 6:14-15), that return is to be expected at God's
chosen time. There is no sense of urgency and no reason to
think that this time chosen by God would be soon. Quite the
opposite seems to be the case. In the support of a variety of
social institutions—like marriage, slavery and political authority, not to mention the church structure of bishops and
deacons recommended in the letter itself for possibly the very
first time—the "Paul" of I Timothy reveals a very different
perspective on "the world as we know it." It is going to
continue! Since this is so, the ways of living in this world that
are most helpful for the preservation of Christian faith and the
existence of the Christian church must be fostered. Marriage is
among these, as the Apostle Paul himself clearly saw but
disregarded because of his eschatological perspective on the
world in general. I Timothy, in contrast, recommends marriage
because it can give structure and stability to the lives of those
who guide the church and represent it to outsiders. It can
contribute significantly to the security, responsibility and
respectability of those who are to live out their full span of
years as Christians *in* "the world as we know it." These

concerns are everywhere evident in I Timothy (2:2, 8-10, 15; 3:2, 4-5, 7, 13; 5:1-14; 6:1). Once again, in studying these letters in the Pauline tradition, we have been drawn into their witness to the complex and organic growth of a living and changing church thinking through its relationship to the gospel of Christ.

We can see another very striking similarity between the Epistle to the Ephesians and the second of the group of letters that we call the Pastorals. II Timothy 1:9-11 contains a very brief statement of the belief that sustains the "Paul" of this letter in his sufferings for the gospel.

> God has saved us and has called us to a holy life, not because of any merit of ours but according to his own design—the grace held out to us in Christ Jesus before the world began but now made manifest through the appearance of our Savior. He has robbed death of it power and has brought life and immortality into clear light through the gospel.

The resemblance between the theology of Ephesians as we have studied it and this encapsuled statement of faith is remarkable. The stress on holiness of life with which it begins strikes one of the predominant ethical notes from Ephesians and recalls perhaps the most important characteristic of the church in Ephesians. What is most reminiscent of the epistle we have just studied, however, is the idea which follows: salvation has been given to us according to the plan of God and grace was held out to us before the world began in Christ Jesus. This is now revealed through the death and resurrected life of the Savior and the preaching of his good news by Paul and others like him. This is the unique theological emphasis of Ephesians within the Pauline tradition, and yet we find it here in II Timothy, so different from Ephesians when considered as a whole. The author of II Timothy does not go on to discuss the plan of God and the place of the church within that plan in detail as the author of Ephesians does. The focus of II Timothy is quite different—a stern warning against false teachers and the presentation of Paul himself as example and guardian of this faith in contrast to these faithless and disputatious teachers. II Timothy is not a theological reflection at all. It depends on brief credal statements like the one cited to express the inherited faith it seeks to transmit and defend. This reliance on creeds that quickly and succinctly recall the faith of the reader is typical of all three Pastoral Epistles and quite consistent with their focus away from theological reflection and toward the effective preservation of theological understanding already attained. Such creeds presuppose that theological thinking like that carried on in the Epistle to the Ephesians has gone before (see I Timothy 2:5-6; 3:16; II Timothy 2:11-12; Titus 3:4-8).

In spite of this reliance on a presupposed theological tradition, however, and in spite of the earnest desire to defend the truth of the faith from any and all attacks and misunderstandings, the Pastoral Epistles can and do exercise a certain amount of judgment even within their received tradition. II Timothy 2:11-12, 16-18 provides us with a very clear illustration of this fact and also an excellent counterpoint to the striking similarity to the theology of the Epistle to the Ephesians we have just been discussing in II Timothy 1:9-12. II Timothy 2:11-12 is a short creed meant to remind us of the faith that cannot be denied by those who hope to obtain the salvation and the eternal glory to be found in Christ Jesus (II Timothy 2:10). It reads

> You can depend on this: If we have died with him we shall also live with him; If we hold out to the end we shall also reign with him.

Timothy is charged to constantly "remind people of these things." Indeed these words do remind us of Paul's own gospel, as it is expressed for example in Romans 5:1-10; 6:3-5; 8:17-19, Philippians 3 as well as many other places. From our earlier study of Colossians and Ephesians we are familiar with the idea of the believer's death with Christ as the source of our hope of life with Christ as a basic part of the Pauline gospel. However, you will remember that Colossians, and especially Ephesians, had a great deal more to say about the mystery of our life with Christ. Recall Ephesians 2:6, for example, "both with and in Christ Jesus he raised us up and gave us a place in heavens." A similar idea is more moderately expressed in Colossians 2:12, "In baptism you were not only buried with him but also raised to life with him because you believed in the power of God who raised him from the dead." It is part of the witness of Colossians and Ephesians within the Pauline tradition that in some mysterious way we are already united with Christ in his resurrection and his glorification. II Timothy 2:16-18 is all the more surprising, therefore, when it says

> Avoid worldly, idle talk, for those who indulge in it become more and more godless, and the influence of their talk will spread like the plague. This is the case with Hymenaeus and Philetus, who have gone far wide of the truth in saying that the resurrection has already taken place. They are upsetting some people's faith.

The contrast between Colossians and Ephesians on the one hand and II Timothy on the other presents the modern reader of the epistles with an opportunity to think about the different viewpoints taken on the question of Christian resurrection and life in and with Christ, and the implications they have for a modern biblical spirituality. Certainly Colossians and Ephesians do not mean to assert against all reasonable evidence to the contrary that Christians have vanished from the earth to be whisked off to heaven with the Lord on the day they came to faith or baptism. Yet we have discussed the concept of a realized resurrection and glorification for Christians through their unity with their resurrected and glorified Lord as one of the most important ideas of the Pauline tradition as it expressed itself in those two closely associated letters. Their theological witness must be taken absolutely seriously, and modern Christians, like their earlier sisters and brothers in faith, can have the confidence that in some mysterious way their salvation in Christ is fulfilled in the present and not simply a hope for the future.

On the other hand, the author of II Timothy tells us very clearly that Christian life is life lived in hope and endurance waiting for the glory of reigning with Christ in the heavens. II Timothy speaks of the future dimension of Christian existence and insists that it not be swallowed up and forgotten in an enthusiasm for the gifts we have already received in Christ. The author of II Timothy speaks to the plain facts of our daily lives as Christians. Here we are: we've died with Christ in baptism and we still must endure our lives in this world—the world as we know it—in the confidence that one day we too will sit with Christ at the right hand of God in power and glory.

There are a number of possible ways to look at the difference between these two strands of the Pauline tradition on this matter. Some of them are more fruitful than others. You might think that Ephesians and II Timothy are opposed to one another on this point and so conclude that we must choose between them, accepting one and abandoning the other. But to do this would be to be unfaithful to the biblical tradition itself, since the New Testament roots of our faith lie in both Colossians/Ephesians and the Pastoral Epistles. Our faith and spiritual life would be impoverished by this choice. You might decide that the author of II Timothy and the author of Ephesians really meant to say the same thing after all; that there is no difference between them. But to do this would be to be unfaithful to the epistles themselves, since we would have to ignore the very specific message that one or the other is trying to send to us across all of these centuries. There really is a difference between saying that we are already glorified with Christ and saying that we hope some day to reign with him following a life of endurance to the end. Our spirituality would be impoverished by the loss of either insight into the meaning of our salvation. Finally, we could allow the wisdom of these early writers who took the Apostle Paul as their teacher to lead us into the mystery of our life in Christ from two quite different directions. Like the reality of the church as a whole, the reality of every individual Christian is mysterious. Each of us *is* what we *cannot possibly be*—raised up to new life, seated at God's right hand with Christ, ruling the universe with him. Yet, paradoxically, each of us *is* what we *appear to be*—living out our lives in the world in endurance and in hope of a new and eternal life when the world as we know it ceases to exist for us as we cease to exist in it at the moment of death. *Together* these letters in the Pauline tradition that we are studying here reveal this profound truth about our own individual existence in Christ. *Together* these letters bear witness to the tension that lies at the heart of the gospel between the *realization* of our salvation and our *hope* of salvation which both exist together, at the same time, in each of us in and through Jesus Christ. Our faith is enriched by reflecting on the mystery our own lives have become in Christ. The distinctive messages of various authors within Paul's tradition permit us to see more clearly this mystery that we are. We will never be able to fully capture and explain this paradox of our own existence, even to ourselves, or reduce it to a simple statement, because in faith and in Christ we as individuals partake of the mystery that is God. The diversity that we frequently find within the New Testament, like the differences we have uncovered and traced throughout this study of Colossians, Ephesians and the Pastoral Epistles, leads us into the paradoxical and inexplicable nature of the divine.

The Real Church:
Patterns of Interactivity Between Church and World According to the Pastoral Epistles

We have already stressed many of the important themes for our study of the spirituality of the Pastoral Epistles in the earlier parts of this chapter. Two of the most important ideas for our purposes here are the very positive point of view taken in each of the Pastoral Epistles toward the world as we know it and the encouragement each provides for fruitful interaction between the church as a whole, and in particular the individual Christian man or woman, and social realities within that world. A third element of the thought of the Pastoral Epistles which has had tremendous consequences for the factual "being Christian" of uncounted numbers of believers throughout the many centuries of Christian history is the practical focus on concrete issues of leadership, morality and structure that the Pastoral Epistles offer to the church of all ages. The Pastoral Epistles tell us how best to solve certain problems, how to provide the church with an organizational foundation that will allow it to continue to exist through time and cultural changes. As individuals each of us needs many things to help us make our lives livable and productive. We need a strong self-identity. We need the security that makes independent activity possible. We need a sense of the past and a vision for the future. We need leadership, role models to provide an example to follow. More than that, we need practical guidelines and sometimes personal guidance to provide advice when we are uncertain and correction when we have gone astray. We need all these things as human beings; we need them as Christians; the church needs them as a community in the world as we know it.

The Pastoral Epistles provide for all of these individual and practical needs of Christians in the church in a way that the letters that we have been studying earlier in this volume do not. Of course, the Pastoral Epistles in themselves do not answer every possible question which might come up in the life of the church. And, the advice provided is sometimes more suitable for the age in which the letters were written than it is for our own time. Still, the author of the Pastoral Epistles did offer effective answers, concrete and specific answers, to the questions of that day, and in doing so issued a call to the church in every age to find its own answers in each new "here and now." Sometimes the guidance of the Pastorals is different from the things that Paul himself said or did, at least as far as we know. Paul does not seem to have appointed presbyters in every town, as Titus is urged to do (Titus 1:5), and we find no evidence in the authentic letters for much of the structure that I Timothy suggests to provide the church with the stability needed in a time of growing numbers and increased social awareness. In the giving of practical advice and the solution of concrete community issues, however, the Pastorals definitely have taken the Apostle Paul himself as their model. Paul devoted large sections of most of his letters to giving just that sort of guidance and correction (Romans 12-16; I Corinthians 1-14; II Corinthians 8-13; Galatians 4-6; Philemon, I Thessalonians and Philippians as a whole).

PAUL AS PARADIGM

The letters of Paul himself also give us very clear precedent for the *way* in which the Pastoral Epistles have chosen to communicate the practical guidance and specific instructions that are their major contribution to the spirituality of the church in all ages. All of the Pastoral Epistles present Paul as the model or exemplar of Christian life. Paul is the perfect Christian person, the perfect Christian leader, and the perfect Christian teacher. It was common in the literature of the day for a writer to offer a kind of self-portrait in order to teach by example the moral exhortation contained in a philosophical letter or ethical treatise.[23] It was also common to choose an example from the past, or even from contemporary events, to serve as a type of either virtue or vice when trying to persuade others to pursue the proper course of action and avoid an incorrect or dishonorable one. The Apostle Paul used this technique frequently. Many examples could illustrate this; we will be satisfied with only one. Paul says in I Corinthians 10:33-11:1 "... just as I try to please all in any way I can by

[23]A recent scholarly study has been devoted to this topic. Benjamin Fiore, S.J., *The Function of Personal Example in the Socratic and Pastoral Epistles.* (Rome: Biblical Institute press, 1986). This is a very technical book and not meant for the general reader. It provided much background material and a viewpoint on the Pastoral Epistles that will influence their interpretation for some time to come.

seeking, not my own advantage, but that of the many, that they may be saved. Imitate me as I imitate Christ." In the preceding chapters, I Corinthians Seven through Ten, Paul had referred to his own behavior many times in exhorting the Corinthians to behave properly in matters of sexuality, liturgy, the support of apostles and ministers, and the eating of meats made available in the marketplace after having been sacrificed in pagan temples. He had even used the experience of Israel in the wilderness in I Corinthians 10:1-13 as an example of the need for perseverance in virtue in spite of God's testing. In verses 6 and 11 Paul mentions explicitly that these events of the past have happened *as an example*. You can see how important the function of paradigm, or example, is elsewhere in Paul's writings as you read I Corinthians 3-4, especially 4:6-13; 7-10; II Corinthians 4-7, especially 6:3-13; 10-13; Galatians 1-2; 4:12-20; 5:7-13 and Philippians 1-2:18; 3-4. The Epistle to the Philippians as a whole is an exhortation to an imitation of Christ's pattern of willing self-sacrifice in acceptance of suffering on the part of the faithful in Philippi based on the paradigmatic experience of Paul himself. It is this aspect of Paul's own letters that is most recognizable in the Pastoral Epistles. Paul is present here as a pattern for the acceptance of salvation in Christ in I Timothy 1:12-16, as an example of the Christian martyr in II Timothy 1:8, 11, 15-18; 2:8-10; 3:11-12; 4:6-18 and as a model for the Christian teacher throughout the Pastorals, but especially in texts like I Timothy 1:3-7, 15, 18-20; 3:14-16; 4:6-16; 6:11-14, 18-21; II Timothy 1:5-8, 11-14; 2:1-2, 7, 14-16; 3:10-17; 4:1-5; Titus 1:1-3, 9-14; 2:1, 8, 15; 3:8-10. In the Pastoral Epistles Paul the Apostle is brought very close to us. He addresses us, through Timothy, as his beloved children (I Timothy 1:2; II Timothy

1:2-5) and teaches us, as a father would, to follow in his footsteps.

Paul as Paradigm for the Experience of Christ

In his authentic letters Paul gives us very little autobiographical information, and none at all that is not meant to illustrate in some way the gospel that he preaches. The texts to read to gather what little information we do have from Paul himself are Galatians 1:12-2:14; Philippians 3:5-7 and Romans 9:1-5. Paul portrays himself as a law-observant Jew, well schooled in the traditions of Israel, zealous for his religious community to the point of persecuting those who denied it—those who were Christians before him, whom Paul perceived as apostates from the true faith of Judaism. This persecutor himself underwent a profound transformation following a "revelation" of God's son, Jesus Christ. Probably Paul refers to a visionary experience of some kind, but he never describes it for us further. What was important to him was that this experience of Christ caused him to join the ranks of the persecuted. More than that, he came to understand that he was called, not only to faith in Jesus Christ, but also to spread that faith among those who had previously been separated from the community and traditions of Judaism, the Gentiles, by revealing Christ in himself. I Timothy 1:12-16 retells part of this story.

> I thank Christ Jesus our Lord, who has strengthened me, that he has made me his servant and judged me faithful. I was once a blasphemer, a persecutor, a man filled with arrogance; but because I did not know what I was doing in my unbelief, I have been treated mercifully, and the grace of our Lord has been granted me in overflowing measure, along with the faith and

love which are in Christ Jesus. You can depend on this as worthy of full acceptance: that Christ Jesus came into the world to save sinners. Of these I myself am the worst. But on that very account I was dealt with mercifully, so that in me, as an extreme case, Jesus Christ might display all his patience, and that I might become an example to those who would later have faith in him and gain everlasting life.

If you have read the texts cited above you can see that this account recalls what Paul himself thought of as a vital part of his life-story. Paul persecuted the church of Christ as a Jew before he had come to faith. Therefore, Paul's salvation came to him as an act of mercy and forgiveness to one who did not in any way merit the gift of faith and conversion on the basis of actions. It is clearly on this idea that I Timothy places the greatest stress.

In fact, the "Paul" of I Timothy seems to place even greater emphasis on it than the Paul of Galatians or Philippians, for example, does. In those authentic letters Paul certainly does allude to his former persecution of the church, but as evidence of his earlier zeal for God, misplaced though it might have turned out to be. He regards this former zeal as one of the things he has sacrificed, or thrown away, for the sake of Jesus Christ. One cannot, or at least does not, sacrifice something that is of no value. In I Corinthians 15:9-10 Paul says

I am the least of the apostles; in fact, because I persecuted the church of God, I do not even deserve the name. But by God's favor I am what I am. This favor of his to me has not proved fruitless. Indeed, I have worked harder than all the others, not on my own but through the favor of God.

Paul certainly saw his persecution of the church as misplaced zeal, as a sin and a mistake, but he regards the zeal for God itself as a good thing. He is even more zealous *for* the church now than he was *against* it formerly, for as an apostle he works *with* the power of God and not against it. Paul would agree with the author of I Timothy that he "did not know what he was doing" in his unbelief, but he does not stress his own sinfulness when discussing his former life.

The author of I Timothy does stress Paul's sinfulness; indeed, Paul is the very worst of those sinners whom Jesus Christ came into the world to save. And this is exactly the point, as our author tells us explicitly. Paul is "an extreme case" in which "Jesus Christ might display all his patience," so that he could be "an example to those who would later have faith in him [Jesus Christ] and gain everlasting life." As is so often the case in the New Testament, the text tells us perfectly clearly what is being said and why it is being said, if only we have the ears to listen to it. Paul is portrayed as the greatest of sinners in order to serve as an example for us! We are certainly among those in the future who have faith in Jesus Christ.

Paul is a paradigm of the gospel itself, first of all. As Paul says in a very early text of his own, it is one of the fundamental statements of the faith in which we stand that "Christ died for our sins" (I Corinthians 15:3). Paul has become an assurance for all of us that Jesus Christ has in fact caused mercy to overflow upon the most sinful of sinners. If he has shown mercy to Paul, who was a "blasphemer, a persecutor, a man filled with arrogance," the Lord will certainly also have mercy on us. Even if we are sinners too, as we all know that we sometimes are, the mercy and love of Christ will surely be given to us. Paul, the worst of sinners, was made a servant of Jesus Christ and judged faithful in his labors. Remember that Paul was the revered apostolic leader of the churches that originally read this letter to Timothy. Surely this is a case of the least becoming the greatest of all. As such, Paul is the assurance of our own hope for forgiveness and everlasting life in Christ. Paul as paradigm in I Timothy speaks to our experience of sinfulness as well as to our hope of redemption. Through this letter as his vehicle, Paul remains almost as close to us today as he must have been to his own child in the faith, Timothy, and is able to instruct and comfort us also.

His example serves as an inspiration for us to abandon our sinful ways and come in faith toward our sure hope of forgiveness and salvation. He serves as a warning too for those in the community, in the first century of its existence as well as today, who remain in sin. This negative kind of paradigm is a bit more subtle than the positive one we have been discussing so far. The Pastorals are all full of instructions of various kinds—for bishops, deacons, women, Christians in general and for Timothy and Titus themselves as representatives of us all. Those who can read this letter know how one should act as a Christian, especially as a leader of the community. Several times individuals are specifically named who are leading others astray by spreading false teachings (I Timothy 1:19-20; II Timothy 1:15; 2:17-18; 4:14). Surely these are the *opposites* of Paul and Timothy or Titus. Those who have received Paul's own instructions, at least in this letter, and persist in "rejecting the guidance of conscience" (I Timothy 1:19), unlike Paul, sin in spite of knowing what they are doing. They have made a "shipwreck of their faith" (I Timothy 1:19). These are "turned over to Satan" by Paul, "so that they may learn not to blaspheme" (I Timothy 1:20). These antitypes of the proper Pauline disciple cannot expect the mercy that Paul received unless they, like Paul, come to the faith that the letter itself presents and, like Paul, cease their blasphemy and their arrogance. Paul stands as a witness against false teachers, calling them to recognize their sin and change their ways. Then Paul, as the example of God's mercy and love for the sinner who is a sinner no more, can show them the way to faithful service in the Lord.

The harshness with which the Pastoral Epistles deal with false teaching sometimes makes readers uncomfortable today. We cannot deny the very critical stance taken in some passages, like II Timothy 3:1-9 or Titus 1:10-16, toward those who disagree with the author. The tone of such passages probably should make us uncomfortable, especially in light of the gospel message as we know it from other parts of the New Testament. For example, Matthew 5:44 instructs Christians to behave with love even toward those who disagree with us, even toward those who really are our enemies! Jesus says, "My command to you is: love your enemies, pray for your persecutors." The Pastoral Epistles do not stress this facet of the gospel. As modern Christians we should not imitate their strident and unforgiving tone, but recognize that it was the result of and a response to a real threat to the community and the gospel message it carried. We can then allow other teachings drawn out of the richness of the New Testament to shape our own response to those with whom we don't agree.

This does not mean, however, that the stand that the Pastoral Epistles take against false teachers is valueless for us. On the contrary, these epistles teach us the valuable lesson that not all ways of preaching the gospel are correct or faithful to its original proclamation, not all ways of acting are allowable and appropriate for Christians. It *does* matter how one behaves and what one thinks in this life in the world and the church as we know them. Some things are right and some things are wrong, and we are called upon to decide between the two. The "Paul" of the Pastorals made very clear decisions in matters of faith and morals. While we might not want to imitate the way these decisions are expressed, we must make our own decisions. The Pastoral Epistles challenge the church, the leaders of the church and each individual within it, to distinguish clearly between what is faithful to the gospel and what is not and to act accordingly with courage and with conviction. This is a message that many Christians want to hear today. They want the truth of the gospel to shine untarnished in the church, and so it should. They want the lives of Christian people to proclaim the gospel message of love and justice, and so they should. The Pastoral Epistles call to us today to strive for truth unmixed with error and love unmixed with dissension and strife, and so we should.

Paul as Exemplar of the Sufferings of Christ

If we look once again at Paul's own letters to discover what his life was like as an apostle preaching the gospel of Jesus Christ, we soon discover that it was a life characterized by suffering for the sake of the gospel and for the sake of his churches. The texts which make this the most clear are I Corinthians 4:9-13 and II Corinthians 6:3-10; 11:16-33; 12:7-13:9, although the theme of his apostolic sufferings is an important strand running through all of Paul's letters. We can see that, like Jesus, Paul was frequently rejected by those he called his own, by the very people from whom he should have received support, comfort, and gratitude. We can see that Paul, like Jesus, endured many hardships and much pain in order to bring the good news of God's forgiveness and love into the world. Paul was conscious of his life as an imitation of Christ in suffering (I Corinthians 11:1; Philippians 2:5-11, 17; 3:7-

11, 17; I Thessalonians 1:6; 2:14-15; 3:1-8).

The tradition that followed Paul and grew out of his writings continued to see him as he had seen himself, as a participant in the sufferings and death of Christ. In the Epistle to the Colossians we can see the beginning of this pseudo-Pauline emphasis, as the "Paul" of Colossians speaks—"Even now I find my joy in the suffering I endure for you. In my own flesh I fill up what is lacking in the sufferings of Christ for the sake of his body, the church." This image of Paul as the suffering apostle, or martyr as he comes to be very soon in non-canonical Christian literature and legend, is very strong in the second letter to Timothy, especially, among the Pastoral Epistles. Although reference to Paul's imprisonment and abandonment occur throughout the letter, perhaps it is expressed most clearly in II Timothy 2:8-10, 3:10-12, and, at the close of the letter, in 4:6-8. We read

> Remember that Jesus Christ, a descendant of David, was raised from the dead. This is the gospel I preach; in preaching it I suffer as a criminal, even to the point of being thrown into chains—but there is no chaining the word of God! Therefore I bear with all of this for the sake of those whom God has chosen, in order that they may obtain the salvation to be found in Christ Jesus and with it eternal glory. . .
>
> You have followed closely my teaching and my conduct. You have observed my resolution, fidelity, patience, love, and endurance, through persecutions and sufferings in Antioch, Iconium, and Lystra. You know what persecutions I have had to bear, and you know how the Lord saved me from them all. Anyone who wants to live a godly life in Christ Jesus can expect to be persecuted. . .
>
> I for my part am already being poured out like a libation. The time of my dissolution is near. I have fought the good fight, I have finished the race, I have kept the faith. From now on a

merited crown awaits me; on that Day the Lord, just judge that
he is, will award it to me—and not only to me, but to all who
have looked for his appearing with eager longing.

Once again, in these texts, Paul speaks to us personally, as if
he were here, now, close enough to touch. He is one like us
who has suffered more and yet emerged victorious into eternal
life. His life has been poured out as a sacrifice for the sake of
preaching the gospel. The reward for this sacrifice is assured by
the resurrection of Jesus Christ which offers salvation and
eternal glory to those who, like Paul, follow his way of the
cross in endurance and faithfulness until the end. A reward is
promised specifically to those for whom the return of the Lord
in glory is the focal point of life. Paul's example is intended to
encourage us as Christians in the midst of the suffering and the
pain that are an inevitable part of our lives. These passages
make it very clear that all Christians are called to share in the
sufferings of Christ and, indeed, cannot and should not try to
avoid doing so.

Does this mean simply the inevitability of death as part of
the "human condition," or the sickness, the disappointment,
and the accidents that are part of life for each and every
person? Surely the example of endurance, faith and reward
offered by Paul and, more than that, by Jesus Christ can
comfort us in our times of pain and struggle. But the message
of II Timothy means more than that. It means that a life lived
in an authentically Christian way cannot be easy and cannot
be comfortable. The "Paul" of II Timothy says that a godly life
will inevitably result in persecution; we must expect it. This is
worth thinking about. The lives, and eventual deaths, of Jesus
and of Paul are evidence to us of the truth of this statement.
But why is this so? This is a question that the Judaeo-
Christian tradition has always wrestled with, as have other

great religious and philosophical traditions in human history.

The answer given by II Timothy depends on much reflection that has gone before and on the actual historical experience of Jesus, Paul and many other Christians who were persecuted for the gospel. The New Testament is full of evidence that many early Christians suffered for their faith, as many Christians and Jews have suffered throughout the centuries and do suffer in our own day. The Christian gospel is a transforming message of love and justice. It is a word about God spoken into a world of sin. To bring justice where there is no justice cannot be easy. To live through love in a cruel world cannot be comfortable. Every one of us has experienced this in small, or possibly larger, ways in our own life. If the gospel of Jesus Christ is taken seriously and if it is allowed to guide our lives and dictate our responses to our neighbors, our interactions with strangers, or our relationships with co-workers, we will be living the godly lives that our author says will call forth persecution. If we respond to anger, not with anger, but a smile and a kind word, we will seem to be fools. If we become more concerned with the starving children of the world than with our own comfort, we will be ridiculed. If we give up our own privileges, or ask that others do so, in order that people of all races can join together as equals in housing, education, or employment, we will be considered dangerous. If we protest against failure to live up to the gospel's call for mercy or equality in Christ within our own churches we will suffer for it. If we do all these things in a public way, we might indeed be persecuted. Yet surely all these things are actions that the gospel demands of us as modern Christians. I am sure that you can think of many more concrete examples.

For Paul, acceptance of the gospel meant abandoning everything that he had—home and synagogue, comfort and security—in favor of constant traveling to preach the message of salvation to strangers who often finally rejected him. He endured criticism even from his friends and from those who thought themselves better than he was, those who might have had more experience or authority than he had. He persevered in this, although he suffered, and the Pastoral Epistles hold him up as a model for each of us to imitate. It may be that we will never do anything so dramatic, although there are certainly real spiritual leaders in our world today who do. The Pastoral Epistles challenge the leadership of the church especially to follow Paul into a ministry of suffering and sacrifice in imitation of Christ. Nevertheless, the challenge is there in our ordinary lives as Christians to let the power of Christ lead us into a "godly life" and to accept the suffering this will entail. We might well reflect on this question: "Why not?" If we accept the challenge to follow a crucified Jesus, and a martyred apostle, the "Paul" of II Timothy assures us that the reward of resurrection and a "crown" await us. If not, is it because we are not willing to risk suffering and so we do not allow the power of the gospel to transform our lives?

Paul as the Guarantor of Christian Tradition

In the preceding section it might have seemed that the author of the Pastoral Epistles was a social innovator, exhorting Christians to change the world through the power of the gospel message. This is not the case. As we have said before, the Pastoral Epistles are supportive of the social world of their time. These letters are more concerned with the respectability and good order of the church itself than with the action of Christians in, or on, the world. But the image of Paul as a sufferer and the concomitant image of the crucified Jesus that it recalls do naturally call forth a response in the direction of social action in modern Christians. In part, this is because of the tendencies in this direction present in our culture and the tremendous needs of the world today that cry out for justice and love expressed in the most concrete actions on behalf of a suffering, impoverished and endangered humanity. In part, too, we were recalling the example of the historical Paul and the earthly Jesus, both of whom aligned themselves with the outcast, the poor and the homeless, both of whom put themselves voluntarily in utter jeopardy to proclaim the mercy of God to an evil world.

But, the "Paul" of the Pastoral Epistles, as he is presented in the most pervasive portrait of him contained in these letters, is not too much concerned with the problems that we face today outside of the church. The "Paul" of the Pastorals is very much concerned with the internal problems of the early church, the most important of which was very obviously a threat to the faith of the church in the form of false teachings. For this reason, our author portrays the apostle as the fountainhead of a line of tradition that is to be handed on to Timothy and Titus, and through them in turn to others who come after them. This tradition is both theological and ethical. This is perhaps the most frequently expressed idea in these letters. We can see it, for example, in I Timothy 3:14-15

> Although I hope to visit you soon, I am writing you about these matters so that if I am delayed you will know what kind of conduct befits a member of God's household, the church of the living God, the pillar and bulwark of truth.

in reference to ethics, the proper conduct for Christians. Paul indeed has been delayed in visiting us in person to tell us these things, but these letters, as well as those he wrote himself, provide us with the guidance we need so that we can live as befits members of God's family. We can see Paul as the source of authentic teaching also in II Timothy 1:13-14:

> Take as a model of sound teaching what you have heard me say, in faith and love in Christ Jesus. Guard the rich deposit of faith with the help of the Holy Spirit who dwells within us.

With Paul standing at the very beginning of the "deposit of faith," its truth is guaranteed by his apostolic authority. Starting with him, this theological tradition, the faith of the church, is passed from generation to generation with the help of those who, in Paul's place, teach it anew in every age. II Timothy begins (1:5-6) with this thought, as Paul speaks, as if directly to us:

> I find myself thinking of your sincere faith—faith which first belonged to your grandmother Lois and to your mother Eunice, and which (I am confident) you also have. For this reason, I remind you to stir into flame the gift God bestowed when my hands were laid on you.

Many of us also inherited our faith from our parents and grandparents. So, the feeling this passage evokes is of a very powerful and intimate link between this "personal tradition" and the apostolic tradition of Paul.

Paul himself is the model for the teachers who succeed him. The letters are full of instructions to Timothy and Titus to follow carefully the example they have seen in him and the teachings they have heard from him. For example, we read some of these in II Timothy 2:1-2, 7, 14-16a:

> So you, my son, must be strong in the grace which is ours in Christ Jesus. The things which you have heard from me through

> many witnesses you must hand on to trustworthy men who
> will be able to teach others. . . . Reflect on what I am saying, for
> the Lord will make my meaning fully clear. . . .
> Keep reminding people of these things and charge them before
> God to stop disputing about mere words. This does no good and
> can be the ruin of those who listen. Try hard to make yourself
> worthy of God's approval, a workman who has no cause to be
> ashamed, following a straight course in preaching the truth.
> Avoid worldly, idle talk. . . .

Two ideas emerge as especially important in these instructions
to Timothy. First, he must reflect on the things he has heard
from Paul and their meaning will become clear to him.
Throughout history the church has endeavored to follow this
directive. In this Biblical Spirituality Series and in this volume
on letters in the tradition of Paul, we are bringing this ongoing
endeavor to expression ourselves. The teachings of the Apostle
Paul heard "through many witnesses," like the pseudo-Pauline
Epistles to the Colossians, to the Ephesians and to Timothy
and Titus, are to be the reliable guide to a church "following a
straight course" in the truth. Second, Timothy must be strong
in handing on the Pauline teaching to those who are "trustworthy," so that they can in turn teach others. This advice was
intended to ensure the endurance of the gospel in the Pauline
churches of the early centuries of the church's existence.

In fact, the organization of church life and the structures of
Christian leadership established in the churches of the Pastoral
Epistles have created the church as we know it. These factors,
not terribly important to the early Christians who wrote other
Pauline epistles like Colossians and Ephesians, nor to Paul
himself because of his hope for an immediate end to the world
we know, have made possible the continued existence of the
community that believes in Jesus Christ as Lord and Son of
God. The perdurance of the church through time has meant

the continued presence of the gospel message in a world which did not end. The Pastoral Epistles do not develop the theological tradition of Paul in new directions. They do, however, bear witness to the development of the church itself in new directions. The choice of leaders for emerging Christianity made in the churches of the Pastorals has led to the preservation of the theological developments in other areas of the Pauline mission. It was probably in churches like that depicted in the first letter to Timothy that the books that we know now as the New Testament were valued and collected and finally approved. Ultimately then, these churches carried the Pauline tradition to us and have brought faith to life in the world again and again. What were these "trustworthy ones" like? What did they do and how did they act? These questions will occupy us in the next section.

LEADERSHIP IN THE PAULINE CHURCH

We have said before that any large group needs organization and leadership in order to survive and to meet the goals and needs of its own community life. Effective leaders and good working structures can provide the self-identity and stability which are as essential for a group as for an individual person. The church that carried the gospel of Christ through time and into ever-widening geographical areas was led by people chosen for qualities calculated to best create security, a positive relationship with the surrounding society and inner harmony for the community. Their primary duty was to teach the tradition about Jesus Christ and our salvation in him handed down from Paul himself. I Timothy 4:13 makes it clear that teaching is the most important thing that Timothy, as the representative of all proper Christian leaders, must do. "Paul" says, "Until I arrive, devote yourself to the reading of Scripture, to preaching and teaching." The importance of the continual study of scripture, in addition to imitation of the apostle and the handing on of his own words, is also underlined here as a primary source for such Christian teaching. Of course, the study of scripture is itself part of an imitation of Paul, since we have seen that his own theology was heavily indebted to the Old Testament. Much the same message is contained in II Timothy 3:14-17, again with an emphasis on the study of scripture as the inspired wellspring of wisdom for understanding the salvation we have received through faith in Jesus Christ.

> You, for your part, must remain faithful to what you have learned and believed, because you know who your teachers were. Likewise, from your infancy you have known the sacred Scriptures, the source of the wisdom which through faith in Jesus Christ leads to salvation. All Scripture is inspired of God and is useful for teaching—for reproof, correction, and training in holiness so that the man of God may be fully competent and equipped for every good work.

We have surely been on the right track in this volume! We have consistently looked back into the Old Testament to understand the meaning of the letters we have studied, and have often brought to light unsuspected levels of meaning. We have looked back to the New Testament letters of Paul himself to help us appreciate the message of the pseudo-Pauline epistles which are the focus of our study here, and the depth, the scope and the variety of the Pauline tradition is visible now in a new way. The Pastoral Epistles place the scriptures at the heart of the study, the preaching and the teaching of the church. Christian leaders, Christian teachers, Christian scholars, and Christian thinkers—and this of course includes all of us—must always turn to the scriptures in order to fully understand their life in Christ. The scriptures lie at the very heart of the teaching of faith. Side by side with this emphasis on the need for the Christian teacher to remain in constant touch with the wisdom of the word of God in the Bible, is a very strong insistence on the good character of the teacher. Living a life filled with the "good works" that must be characteristic of those who believe is just as necessary as is absolute faithfulness to the scriptures and the apostolic tradition.

The first letter to Timothy and the one to Titus give us remarkably complete descriptions of the qualities and qualifications necessary for the leaders of the church in their day—bishops, presbyters and deacons—in passages like I Timothy 3:1-7, 8-13 and Titus 1:5-6, 7-9. The description of the proper bishop[24] in I Timothy 3:1-7 can serve as an example of the kind of life in "good works" required at this time of one who led, guided, and cared for the church.

> You can depend on this: whoever wants to be a bishop aspires to a noble task. A bishop must be irreproachable, married only once, of even temper, self-controlled, modest, and hospitable. He should be a good teacher. He must not be addicted to drink. He ought not to be contentious but, rather, gentle, a man of

---

[24]The bishop to whom the letter to Timothy refers is not quite the same official person as the one we think of when we hear the term today, in charge of a number of individual churches over a large geographical area. The early bishop was more like a pastor, in our terminology. For a discussion of varous ministries and offices in the early church, see Joseph T. Lienhard, S.J., *Ministry*. Message of the Fathers of the Church 8 (Wilmington, Delaware: Michael Glazier, Inc., 1984).

peace. Nor can he be someone who loves money. He must be a good manager of his own household, keeping his children under control without sacrificing his dignity; for if a man does not know how to manage his own house, how can he take care of the church of God? He should not be a new convert, lest he become conceited and thus incur the punishment once meted out to the devil. He must also be well thought of by those outside the church, to ensure that he does not fall into disgrace and the devil's trap.

Clearly the bishop is the "father" in the "family" of God on earth. He has all the qualities of a good citizen and a good husband and father. He should be gentle, modest, hospitable, moderate, well organized, and respectable. In the portrait of the bishop in the Pastoral Epistles we see a quiet and dignified man of God,[25] a "man of peace" whose job it is to care for God's children and manage God's household as well as his own.

It is just this kind of leader who was able to give the church the peace and quiet, the security, which it needed to thrive as it did in the early centuries of our era. This leader is not

[25]It is certainly true that the candidates for the "noble task" of bishop in the church of I Timothy are indeed men. It is well known that the Pastoral Epistles, especially I Timothy, contain several negative statements about women and the behavior of women in the church (I Timothy 2:12-15; 5:11-15; II Timothy 3:6-7). We have not treated these passages in this volume since they are on the one hand part of the typical mirroring of the accepted social patterns of "the world," and on the other hand not especially beneficial for the development of a contemporary biblical spirituality that speaks to modern culture not in sympathy with these patterns in this case. This negativity toward women is not an aspect of the spirituality of the Pastorals that we should imitate today. For a fascinating literary and historical inquiry into the possible intra-church causes for this subordinationist and critical stance toward women in the community of the Pastoral Epistles, see Dennis Ronald MacDonald, *The Legend and the Apostle* (Philadelphia: The Westminster Press, 1983).

particularly dynamic; we find no firebrand or missionary here. Remember that by the time the Pastorals were written the first missionary period of the Christian movement was past. The need to stay at home and manage the affairs of a large church in a period of steady local growth called for a new kind of leadership for a new kind of church. The bishop in the Pastorals is a family man. Remember that the church from its earliest days was a "household" church. Its meetings and liturgies were held in the homes of its first and founding members, or possibly in the home of whoever had the largest house! The family imagery that we see developing here is a natural outgrowth from these beginnings. As you walk into the church of the Pastoral Epistles, you walk into God's house. The bishop of the Pastorals is a good citizen. He is respected by outsiders. His respectability lent respectability to the church. We have already mentioned the positive view taken in the Pastorals toward interaction with the world outside the church. We see this as an important factor again here. We have noted as well the reasons for this attitude, so often visible here (I Timothy 2:1-2; 3:7; 5:14; 6:1; Titus 2:5, 8, 10) and generally absent from Paul's own letters. In order to survive in the world in which it was inevitably immersed, the church needed to be *allowed to* survive. The good character of its leaders attested to the good character of its members. The good character of its members attested to the truth and value of the faith they professed. And so, over time, the gospel could come to us!

The Pastoral Epistles seem to some to be authoritarian and polemic documents, full of invective and directives—do this! you may not do that! He is wrong and she is wrong! Do not listen to them! In part, this is true. When one sees the reason for this impulse toward good order, discipline and the preservation of the truth of faith, however, one can more easily understand and value it as a necessary response to the needs of the church of that time. Anyone who lives in a large family or is responsible for the care of a large number of people knows about the need for order and discipline in such a group. Any one of us who has been in a totally unfamiliar and threatening situation has longed for the security that can come from being part of a group with a strong leader. If we can remember or empathize with these emotions, we can begin to feel as Christians felt when the Pastorals were written. The world that the church lived in during the late first and second centuries was diverse and threatening. A new identity had to be forged. The gospel of salvation had to be preserved. And these things were done by the good and holy people who carried the Pauline tradition into the world of the second century.

We have focused on the leaders of these people of God's family, because there is a very heavy emphasis on leadership in the Pastoral Epistles. However, the letters also contain instructions and wisdom for the individual members of the household, practical guidance that those who "aspired to the noble task" of leadership also followed as a matter of course. We will conclude our discussion of the letters to Timothy and Titus with the images of Christian life that they offer us and the virtues they require of those who seek to live in "good conscience and sincere faith" (I Timothy 1:4).

TRAINING IN FAITH—CHRISTIAN VIRTUE IN HOPE OF ETERNAL LIFE

The description of the bishop in I Timothy 3:1-7 calls into the reader's mind images of solidity and security—good

father, upstanding citizen, prudent householder—but another
primary image of Christian life for everyone—Timothy included—is an image of action and effort. For the Pastoral
Epistles in general, the day-to-day life of one who has faith in
Christ and hopes for eternal life and glory with him is like an
athletic contest—especially a race or battle—for which we
train and in which we compete hoping for the victory merited
by our perseverance and our strength. Paul himself uses this
imagery several times in his own letters, in I Corinthians
9:24-27; II Corinthians 10:3-5; Philippians 3:12-15. Paul thinks
of himself most frequently as a runner, who trains to have the
strength to finish the race and be the winner. His sufferings in
the course of his apostolic mission are the exercises he must
perform. Resurrected life with Christ will be his crown of
victory if he has the strength to finish the course and win the
race. Paul himself constantly emphasizes that the source of his
ability to do all this is God's strength rather than his own (II
Corinthians 3:4-5; 11:30; 12:10; 13:3-4).

The phrase "training in faith," taken from I Timothy 1:4,
introduces this idea at the very beginning and sets a tone that
is constant in all of these epistles. The exercise demanded by
our "training" as Christians is explained immediately. It is the
"spiritual exercise" of "love that springs from a pure heart, a
good conscience, and sincere faith." The same idea is expressed
in I Timothy 4:7-8,

> Train yourself for the life of piety, for while physical training is
> to some extent valuable, the discipline of religion is incalculably
> more so, with its promise of life here and hereafter.

and appears again, along with military and agricultural imagery,
in II Timothy 2:3-7.

It is sometimes amazing how directly the Bible can speak to

the contemporary scene, although at other times its meaning is difficult to apply to our world because the text is dealing with a situation completely unknown or foreign to us. For example, most Americans under the age of forty have very little experience of foreign domination or exile that would allow the words of warning or comfort of the Old Testament prophets to speak to them directly. Similarly, the eating or not eating of meat offered in pagan temples is absolutely no problem for us, so analogies must be found in our lives in order for Paul's teachings about this in I Corinthians, Chapter Ten, to have any meaning for us at all. This time, however, II Timothy is speaking directly, if not intentionally, to modern life especially in the United States when it recommends that an equal amount of time and care be devoted to spiritual life, as is spent on the cultivation of physical life. Anyone living in America during the past decade is certainly aware that the cultivation of physical fitness has become an obsession in our society. Hours and hours are devoted each day to jogging, "working out," swimming and similar activities. The body is disciplined through diets and exercise. This is something we have in common with ancient Greek society, in which the care of the physical body was important and time was spent in the gymnasium as a regular part of the social life of the city.

The goal of all this "training" is the perfection and prolongation of physical life. Physical imperfection is abhorred. No one can deny that such physical exercise is "to some extent valuable." But one could ask, as the author of II Timothy probably would, whether the same amount of time and effort each day is devoted to the cultivation and enhancement of spiritual life. Is spiritual imperfection abhorred? Do we care as much, even as Christians, about our eternal life with God as we do about our life on earth and the physical aspect of our existence? As a society, we would have to answer, "No." Would even Christians answer in the negative? If so, according to the Pastoral Epistles, there is something wrong with the way we look at ourselves and with the way our faith is integrated into our life "in the world." Hours of prayer and study of the scriptures should stand beside the time we spend on physical exercise. Hours of service to our community of faith in whatever capacity—leadership and service in worship, teaching, charity and filling the needs of others—are at least as important for our existence as Christian people as jogging is for our cardiovascular system! What kind of life do we want to make sure lasts forever? We cannot prolong our physical existence forever, no matter how hard we try. But we can live forever with God if, our author tells us, we begin our "godly life" here and now and strengthen our faith and love day by day. The "Paul" of II Timothy says "if one takes part in an athletic contest, he cannot receive the winner's crown unless he has kept the rules" (II Timothy 2:5).

After the almost mystical theological reflections on the church and our existence in Christ in the Epistle to the Ephesians, this might seem a rather pedestrian kind of imagery to use to describe our hope as Christians. The New Testament and the Pauline tradition within it, however, speak to our whole being at all levels, from the most practical level of our daily lives to the highest level our minds can reach. We need to be able to look at our ordinary lives with the eyes of faith. We need answers to mundane, as well as theological, questions. How should we organize our lives with an authentically Christian set of values? What should we do in the here-and-now?

The Pastoral Epistles give us this kind of advice. There are several ideas that seem to come up often in the letters, things that were particularly important in the mind, or the church, of the author. One of these is prayer. The instruction to pray is the first specific one in the first letter, in I Timothy 2:1-4.

> First of all, I urge that petitions, prayers, intercessions, and thanksgiving be offered for all men, especially for kings and those in authority, that we may be able to lead undisturbed and tranquil lives in perfect piety and dignity. Prayer of this kind is good, and God our savior is pleased with it, for he wants all men to be saved and come to know the truth.

The placement of this passage as the first in a long series of instructions underlines the importance of prayer in the lives of these Christians. We have already noted that constant study of the scriptures and reflection on the teachings of Paul are part of the spiritual training that makes these early believers fit for the hope of eternal life. Prayer, both in the context of liturgy and in private, must be an important part of our lives as Christians if we want to follow in the footsteps of our Pauline ancestors.

Several details of this general admonition to pray are also interesting. First of all, the Christian community of the Pastorals is told to pray for those *outside* of their group, especially for public officials and political authorities. This is a clear instance of the positive relationship that is being built in these letters between the church and the world. Second, such prayer serves a purpose for the increase of faith or piety. This community is in a way praying for itself, praying that it be allowed to exist in peace within the surrounding society and its structures, protected by the authorities for whom it offers intercession and thanksgiving to God. Finally, there is the hope in the Pastoral Epistles that all of humanity will come to faith through the church. In the Pastorals this is not a theoretical or philosophical consequence of the universality of the creative and redemptive act of God, as it was in Ephesians for example. In the Pastoral Epistles, the universal salvation of all of humanity is a practical hope to be realized through the witness of the church to the truth and salvation of its God. This universal salvation can be made a reality not least through the efficacious prayer of the church on behalf of the world, but also through the proclamation of the truth in the form of creeds (as in I Timothy 2:5-6) and in the dignified and pious behavior of its members.

The proper use of wealth also seems to have been of great importance to the author of the Pastorals. II Timothy 6:7-10, 17-19 has a very negative opinion of money and of its possible value in the attainment of salvation.

> We brought nothing into this world, nor have we the power to take anything out. If we have food and clothing we have all that we need. Those who want to be rich are falling into temptation and a trap. They are letting themselves be captured by foolish and harmful desires which drag men down to ruin and destruction. The love of money is the root of all evil. Some men in their passion for it have strayed from the faith, and have come to grief amid great pain. . . .
> Tell those who are rich in this world's goods not be proud, and not to rely on so uncertain a thing as wealth. Let them trust in the God who provides us richly with all things for our use. Charge them to do good, to be rich in good works and generous, sharing what they have. Thus will they build a secure foundation for the future, for receiving that life which is life indeed.

Obviously, there was a problem having to do with the use of money in the church to which this letter was sent. Perhaps becoming a Christian made it difficult to do the things necessary to make money, as it does today if what is required is dishonesty or the callous use of other people as if they were a commodity rather than our brothers and sisters. Perhaps there was envy or partiality within the church on the basis of wealth. Perhaps those with worldly goods to share refused to do so, thereby failing in their obligation to the unity of the community and its support. Whatever was happening in the author's church, the advice that we can take from the letter is clear enough. Just as physical training cannot provide us with spiritual life, or even endlessly prolong our life in this world, money and riches cannot buy for us a "life which is life indeed." Wealth is not intrinsic to us, and can only provide things which are of no ultimate value. The goods which preoccupy and fascinate the rich may draw attention away from the words of salvation. We are familiar enough with this temptation to recognize the truth of the warning we read in I Timothy. The only good that can come from money for our author comes from giving it away, sharing it with others.

Finally, throughout the Pastoral Epistles we can encounter exhortations to perseverance and steadfastness in faith and in virtue, no matter what the cost. We are to follow the example of Jesus himself—something we have not been urged to do very frequently in these Pauline letters whose focus is usually on the heavenly Christ rather than the earthly Jesus. However, I Timothy 6:13-14 urges us to stand fast as Jesus did when faced with the threat of death.

> Before God, who gives life to all, and before Christ Jesus, who in bearing witness made his noble profession before Pontius Pilate, I charge you to keep God's command without blame or reproach until our Lord Jesus Christ shall appear.

Christian virtue is not something that comes easily, nor should we expect it to be. The Pastorals call us all to stand firm and remain constant, as they instruct Timothy to "stay with this task whether convenient or inconvenient" (II Timothy 4:2) until the Lord comes again or we go to be with him. Only those who finish the race can hope for the crown of victory.

In reading through the Pastoral Epistles some attitudes and characteristics stand out for the reader as particularly typical of Christians in these churches. The church is to be free of anger and dissension (I Timothy 2:8, 6:4-5), Christians are to be quiet and modest (I Timothy 2:9), courteous to all (Titus 3:2), serious-minded and pure of heart (I Timothy 3:11, 5:2; II Timothy 2:22). They are to treat each other with respect and gentleness, like members of a single family—fathers, mothers, sisters and brothers to one another (I Timothy 5:1-2; II Timothy 2:24-25). They must support their members who lack any way of supporting themselves, as would be the case for widows with no children or grandchildren to provide for them, just as they would provide for their own relatives (I Timothy 5:3-16). Hospitality toward strangers is highly valued (I Timothy 3:2; 5:10; Titus 1:8), as is impartiality and lack of prejudice within the community itself (I Timothy 5:21). None of these virtues is surprising, but taken as a whole they create a portrait of a Christian people that embodies and expresses the ideal of love in day-to-day living, working through salvation in a life of good works, not limited to those inside the group but done for the sake of outsiders as well. The Christians of the Pastorals are good people, people you would like to know—in fact, they are very much like people you do know! They are like millions of Christians today—the old devoted pastor who looks on his parish as his family, the housewife who organizes the pot-luck supper for the church each year, the widow who plays the organ every Sunday, the young teacher who is in charge of showing the children how to say their prayers. The list could go on and on. The Christians of the Pastoral Epistles are ordinary people, just like us in many ways. Like us, they have their faults. They're too severe with those who don't share their opinions. They're too ready to "get along" with society rather than change it. They tend to repeat the things they believe rather than think about them too much. In recognizing them as our brothers and sisters, we can forgive them for these shortcomings, since we too have flaws. But, they gave us a church that was secure enough to grow. They preserved the truth of the gospel for us in spite of persecution. For most of us, they are our closest relatives in the ancient world. In their church, we recognize our own.

Modern Spirituality in Light of the Pastorals

If we ask, at the end of this reflection on the Pastoral Epistles, what meaning we, as contemporary Christians, find in these particular letters for the enrichment of our spiritual lives, the answer will be different from the response to the same question following our study of the other letters in the Pauline tradition treated in this small volume. In our discussion of these later New Testament examples of the teaching tradition of the Apostle Paul, we have been led into an encounter with the wealth of theological insight, spiritual comfort and practical guidance that is available to us in the great variety of the biblical witness to the truth of our common faith in God and Jesus Christ and to our common life in the Spirit. The Bible, both the Old Testament and the New Testament, speaks to us at all levels of our being and in all aspects of our lives. We are nourished by the study of the scriptures, so strongly urged upon us by the Pastoral Epistles

themselves, in many ways—intellectually, morally, emotional-
ly and in the very practical daily conduct of our lives. This
multifaceted appeal of the biblical tradition is a function of the
diversity of the biblical writers and writings themselves, and is
a mirror of the complexity of our own reality as human beings
created in the image of God. Our lives are lived on many levels
at once—we think, we know, we believe, and we feel individually, we work within the equally important and necessary
physical and communal aspects of our lives, and we do these
things in the context of a social and physical universe that is in
some ways independent of us, though not independent of
God. The Bible reflects on and teaches us about all these
aspects of human existence, even as it reveals the mystery of
God. We have tried to emphasize this interplay of various
levels of meaning within the New Testament books we have
discussed throughout this volume.

The Pastoral Epistles in particular approach us at the
practical, individual, physical and social levels. The special
strength of these letters is the help they provide for us as
individual Christians in our relationships within society and
in the conduct of our lives as we live them in the world as we
find it. The Pastorals also provide practical guidance for the
church as a group. They provide patterns for the interactions
of different individuals—bishops, deacons, widows, teachers—
designed to strengthen the group as a whole and provide for
peaceful and mutually beneficial and satisfactory relationships
in church life. The Pastoral Epistles counsel us about how to
keep the truth of the gospel vital to our lives, in our communities, and for our world by ordering our behavior, organiz-
ing our churches and passing on our traditions in ways that
will enable the church to endure. The church of the Pastoral
Epistles is a church conscious of its existence as a real social

body and of the special needs of its life *as* a society and *in* a society. The church of the Pastorals is a church conscious of its apostolic heritage and of its mission to preserve and transmit it to the churches of the future. The ways in which the author of the Pastorals chose to accomplish these goals were ways especially effective in the earliest days of Christianity. We can see how effective the structure of leadership and teaching authority was, for example, in the very fact that the truth of the gospel is still proclaimed by a Christianity that has endured for many, many centuries to embrace more peoples than the believers of that time could possibly have imagined. Sometimes our own answers might be different, as we meet new problems and need to discover our own ways of passing on our traditions and structuring our communities in inter-action with a world that has changed considerably since the first or second century of our era. This is as it should be, since the Pastoral Epistles themselves represent a changed and, in some ways, a specialized way of looking at authority and church life in Pauline communities, especially when viewed against the background of Paul's own writings and other epistles like Colossians and Ephesians. Yet, the fundamental attitudes of these epistles remain as valid today as they were at the very beginning of the church's life. Several are especially valuable for us.

The most important of these fundamental, practical insights that are characteristic of the letters to Timothy and Titus is that faith in Christ can and should exist within a positive relationship between the believer and the church as a whole on the one hand and the social and physical universe on the other. As Christians we know, just as these Christians of the late first century knew, that we *must* live our lives as Christians in the same world in which we live our lives as parents, workers, teachers, merchants, bankers, or husbands and wives. There can be no disjunction between our faith, our life in the church and the rest of our lives. In the Pastoral Epistles, family and social relationships are brought into the realm of the gospel and woven into the fabric of life and belief, church and world, seen as an organic whole. We learn from these letters that we do not need to be alienated from the world around us to be Christian. Far from it! For the author of the Pastorals, the church, and the individuals who are part of it, should value the social and political world they live in and can be a positive force within the world (I Timothy 2:1-4).

We have seen the "Paul" of these epistles reach deep into the Old Testament tradition to reappropriate the very basic biblical insight that all of God's creation is good and should be received with gratitude and rejoicing (I Timothy 4:3-5; 5:23). We have also seen a respect for the ordinary relationships of family life and a willingness to bring them into the life of the church itself as a force for stability and the nurturing of all who are members of God's family (I Timothy 3:4-7, 12; 5:1-5, 8-10, 16). Finally, we have heard the "Paul" of II Timothy describe his life of labor for the gospel as a contest, a race or a prize fight, just as Paul himself had talked about the "training" he had to undergo to be able to finish his race. We can identify with him, since each of us has experienced the constant effort, struggle and even hardship of life, especially insofar as our lives are devoted to the challenge of bringing the truth and love of the gospel message to full expression day by day. In all these ways the Pastoral Epistles speak to our own experiences as individuals and as church in a more pointed and more prag-matic way than do the other letters we have studied.

The presentation of Paul in the Pastoral Epistles is also important for us today in several ways. As each of these epistles opens and closes, as indeed throughout the many instructions and warnings each contains, the Apostle seems to come very close to us, as if we ourselves were his fellow-workers and beloved children of so long ago. As Christians standing today far along a chain of tradition that extends back through these epistles all the way to Paul himself, we might feel very distant from our origins, rather lost and certainly at a disadvantage in comparison with those who first believed and who followed the Lord or Paul himself and learned the truths of our common faith directly from them. The Pastoral Epistles assure us, however, that we are just as close as they were to the foundations of our belief through the witness of those teachers who have faithfully carried on and delivered the message of salvation we have heard from the beginning. The letters themselves, as well as the other writings of the New Testament, as they bring Paul himself close to us in an almost personal way also bring the basic apostolic witness to the gospel close to us. The creation of a line of men and women charged with faithful witness to the truth, coupled with the formulation of the many credal statements contained in the Pastorals, gives us the same secure foundation that was so important in the early centuries.

Just as early Christians needed a model to follow in the life of persecution and witness that was frequently their lot, we need a model today. Paul is our inspiration via these letters, just as he was theirs. Just as these early Christians needed leaders who could be trusted with the care of their congregations, so do we. In the Pastoral Epistles, we have guidelines for choosing the qualities which should be characteristic of them. The most important qualifications are holiness, responsibility and the gentleness and selflessness necessary to care for others with courage but without arrogance. Similarly, the primary characteristics of the church as a whole in these letters is utter faithfulness to the truth and the peace that comes from impartiality and selfless love. Virtues that promote peace and unity for the sake of the common good are recommended here—gentleness, modesty, temperance, hospitality, truthfulness, purity, devotion to duty and perseverance in the truth. Vices that destroy the common good for the sake of the individual gain are strongly rebuked—contentiousness, greed, laziness, prejudice, envy, slander, and injustice. Just as these early Christians needed to be reminded of the kind of life that must flow naturally from our profession of faith, so must we. Faith is not something that can be only part of our existence. Our faith must touch every area of our lives, creating the church as a society in which we profess our faith together and from which we reach out into the world around us with the message of God's love.

The profound sense of our common faith and the emphasis on our ancient tradition that is characteristic of the Pastoral Epistles is also extremely valuable for today's Christian. Our age is plagued with uncertainty; we are not living in a time of complacency, comfortable with our past and certain of our future. Sometimes it can seem that we are uncertain of everything—including truths that once seemed so unshakable, even the continued existence of life on our planet! In contrast to this, when we read the Pastorals we find a strong impulse to preserve the past and find certainty and security in our faithfulness to it. The "Paul" of the Pastorals understands our need to constantly affirm our faith together. He recognizes the danger in unrestrained change and speculation. He knows our fear of losing our footing and becoming detached from the wellspring of our faith in the scriptures and the traditions of the apostles and teachers of the past. The emphasis in the

Pastoral Epistles responds to a very profound and legitimate need we all feel for a strong self-identity as Christians, for a solid foundation for faith in the apostolic preaching about Christ and for a sense of community undisturbed by error and dissension. These epistles tell us that when we look for these things we are on the right track. We have a strong and very old tradition; we should seek our secure foundation there. We should reject opinions that are radically inconsistent with that tradition and behavior that tends to destroy our unity rather than to build it up.

Yet the Pastoral Epistles themselves speak against any narrowness in this preservation of tradition. They do not warrant a simplistic or easy answer through recourse to the past. In challenging us to hold fast to the teaching of the Apostle Paul, for example, the letters to Timothy and Titus do not limit us but send us into all the other letters in the Pauline tradition, those we have studied in this volume as well as those written by the Apostle himself. In their uncompromising demand that we search for the apostolic teaching and live our lives in complete faithfulness to it, the Pastoral Epistles are directing us to the gospels, the sermons of Hebrews, the Epistles of John, and the Book of Revelation—all of which stand in the eyes of the church on the firm foundation of apostolic witness. As the Pastorals exhort us to study the scriptures and reflect on them as a source of wisdom for the church, they are encouraging us to read and study the Old Testament scriptures as well. We have seen the importance of the Old Testament for Paul and those who followed him. Finally, when the "Paul" of the Pastorals assures us that we should listen to those who teach faithfully, and in all truthfulness, the tradition that has been handed down, he is asking us to listen to those within our own churches who do just that—not only our leaders, although they have a special charge to teach in submission to the original statements of our faith, but to all Christians who search for the wisdom of God in the scriptures and proclaim our common faith in Jesus Christ as Son of God and savior of the world, just as the earliest believers and the apostles themselves once did. In short, the idea of the preservation of tradition so important in the Pastoral Epistles has a two-fold function for us. It grounds our faith, our community and our very selves in the certainty of the past and the word of God in Jesus Christ and those who first proclaimed his mystery and his message. But, it also opens up for us the riches of the whole biblical tradition—the multifaceted prism in which we can glimpse the face of God and hear the word of God spoken in many human voices to each and every one of us.

Conclusion

This study of biblical spirituality devoted to five letters in the Pauline tradition has been a difficult one in one significant respect. As we anticipated from the very beginning, in dealing with letters written by at least three different authors, we have studied not one, but several, distinct "spiritualities." That is, we have studied the unique ways in which at least three disciples of the Apostle Paul used his preaching about salvation in the Lord Jesus Christ to create a synthesis in and through which the world, the community and the self could be understood in their relationship to God. We have tried to be faithful to the special interests and contributions of each of these authors within the totality which is the biblical witness to faith. In the first chapter of this study, our focus was primarily on God's relationship to the world in Christ, and the way we can make this relationship part of our own spirituality of hope today. In the second chapter our focus shifted toward the community in its relationship to God in Christ. We sought a deepened contemporary self-identity for the church in the profound theological witness of the Epistle to the Ephesians to our eternal destiny in Christ. In the third chapter, our attention turned to the individual and the church as examples of life lived through faith within the practical and social world of experience. Perhaps we have found some guidelines here for our own task of integrating our Christian self-identity and the political, ecclesial, social and familial roles each of us plays during a lifetime. Although the primary interest in each major section of this study has reflected, not only the primary interest of an individual author, but also one of the major facets of spirituality itself, in fact these interests have not been exclusive in any section or for any author. God, Christ, world, church and individual are co-existing in a dynamic, multiform and constantly changing relationship, for each author and for each of us. So, no part of the synthesis that is spirituality has been completely absent from any of the letters we have studied, or from any part of this book.

The challenge of treating a variety of "spiritualities" in a single volume has been a very fruitful one. It has led us to encounter the great riches of the New Testament at a variety of levels and has been a convincing illustration of several very important aspects of any truly biblical spirituality. For example, since the New Testament spirituality is so various and can and does allow for considerable difference in emphasis and view-point, we can be sure that contemporary Christian spirituality is likely also to be extremely diverse, with syntheses as numerous as there are individuals striving to integrate their faith, thoughts, and unique life experiences, while preserving their unity with one another in Christ. Since we have seen different Pauline churches in the very earliest times develop a stronger faith in Christ as they responded to challenges of false worship or false teaching, we can have confidence that we as contemporary Christians can respond to similar challenges which will surely come, and emerge with an even brighter hope and a clearer vision of the meaning of life in Christ. As we have observed disciples of the Apostle Paul develop new understandings of the relationship between Christ and the church, or between the church and the world, because of changes occurring within and around their communities through time, we realize that we too can welcome and absorb change while remaining completely faithful to the roots and source of our faith in Christ.

In the course of our study of Colossians, Ephesians and the Pastoral Epistles, we have encountered many ideas. The Epistle to the Colossians, for example, proclaims the divinity of Christ and his creative, sustaining and redeeming power over all of reality. This faith in Christ and this vision of his authority over *our* world have the power to give us an absolute hope—a hope not naive, but absolute because it is grounded in the reality and revelation of God. The Epistle to the Ephesians discloses the height and breadth and depth of our unity with Christ as a community and the sharing in his reality that is our only life and salvation. Reflecting on the mystery of our own being in the Lord, we are called to become what we already are—one in Christ, holy and blameless before God and joined together in love. The Pastoral Epistles take us into their world in order to show us how to live in our world. They challenge us as individuals to love the world as we find it and yet be a leavening force in converting that world to God. They appeal to us to be a church without bitterness, controversy and dissension living in gentleness, good order and complete faithfulness to the word of God.

But this volume has not been about ideas only. We have seen not only *what* several New Testament authors thought, but *how* they thought. We have seen the way that each Pauline author has constantly looked back into the Old Testament and into the writings of the Apostle Paul in order to articulate the meaning of both faith and experience. We have seen how the Epistle to the Colossians responded to false teaching by even deeper reflection on the truth of the Pauline gospel. We have seen how both the Epistle to the Colossians and the Epistle to the Ephesians made use of contemporary secular thought to express the mystery of Christ for new generations of Christians. We have seen in the Pastoral Epistles that the world can be embraced and previous hopes for the immediate return of the Lord can be transformed as experience leads to new conclusions. These letters in the Pauline tradition offer ideas to contemporary Christians, ideas with the power to transform lives. But, they also offer models, patterns for how to think, how to love and how to live. They urge the preservation of tradition even as they reveal their own creativity in communicating it. Their varied yet integrated witness to faith in Christ is a mirror of the dynamism of Christian life itself. Finally, this is what is most truly characteristic of a biblical spirituality—it is the spirituality of a *living tradition*. What a paradoxical phrase! We are called to look back always into that tradition, and have done so here with these letters which come to us from authors who in turn wrote by looking back into their own Pauline tradition. We have found a constantly self-renewing source of insight, strength and inspiration. Yet we are called also to live as we see the Christians who wrote these letters living—thinking, feeling and responding to our world as they did to theirs. We must preserve and we must constantly express anew—as they did. Following these patterns and reflecting on these ideas, both the legacy of the biblical tradition itself, it is our task to create a truly contemporary, yet authentically biblical, spirituality today.

BIBLICAL INDEX

BIBLICAL INDEX

OLD TESTAMENT

NEW TESTAMENT